I love this book: it's like a ___ you can dip into for wisdom,
encouragement—and lots of belly laughs. Essential reading for clergy kids, families—
and everyone who wants to support them.
EMMA SCRIVENER, BLOGGER AND AUTHOR OF *A NEW NAME* (IVP, 2012)

Nell Goddard's first book is just like Nell Goddard herself: funny, caring and wise. She
faces up to the challenges of family life in ministry honestly but without bitterness,
which makes the book moving, and she shares its hopes and joys, which means that
it is deeply inspiring. If you are a clergy child or a clergyperson with children, this
book will offer you comfort, food for thought and practical advice.
SEAN DOHERTY, TUTOR, ST MELLITUS COLLEGE

By combining humorous anecdotes with deeply vulnerable insight, this book
encourages each of us (whether we're clergy children or not) to trust God, lifting our
eyes to the Father who loves us abundantly. Nell invites us, with all the gentleness
and love of a friend, to lay down our struggles before Jesus and to listen to his still,
small voice of peace. Everyone who reads Nell's words will find grace reflected and
overflowing, helping us to draw closer to God as we walk with him.
HANNAH FYTCHE, AUTHOR OF *GOD'S DAUGHTERS* (BRF, 2016)

Musings of a Clergy Child is essential reading for clergy children and parents. It's
perfect for anyone who grew up in a Christian home who has lost their identity or
faith along the way. A happy combination of funny stories, raw, honest prayers, and
pastoral wisdom. Nell Goddard's writing is a rare treat of dry wit, bracing honesty,
passion and compassion. What shines through her writing is the simple beauty of
a faith honed by challenge, heartbreak and perseverance. Highly recommended.
TANYA MARLOW, AUTHOR

This book is written with honesty, humour, wisdom and integrity, offering an insight
into the often complex business of growing up in a vicarage. Nell has lived this
first-hand. She offers a combination of playful observations, wise advice and deep
reflections. It will challenge, encourage and comfort.
KATE WHARTON, VICAR OF ST GEORGE'S, EVERTON AND ASSISTANT NATIONAL LEADER OF
NEW WINE

Nell Goddard takes the lid off vicarage life and reveals the life of a clergy child to be
anything but a sheltered one. With tenderness and insight she describes the rich and
rare mix of holy, human experience which shaped her growing up. Her faith journey
so far has been remarkable, painful, joyful, very much her own and shot through
with instances of how God and life, in her words, 'intersect in the most beautiful of
ways'.
ROSEMARY LAIN-PRIESTLEY, ARCHDEACON FOR THE TWO CITIES

The Bible Reading Fellowship
15 The Chambers, Vineyard
Abingdon OX14 3FE
brf.org.uk

The Bible Reading Fellowship (BRF) is a Registered Charity (233280)

ISBN 978 0 85746 546 7
All rights reserved
First published 2017
10 9 8 7 6 5 4 3 2 1 0

Text © Nell Goddard 2017
This edition © The Bible Reading Fellowship 2017
Cover images © Nell Goddard, © Thinkstock, © iStock, © Benjamin Ealovega

The author asserts the moral right to be identified as the author of this work

Acknowledgements
Unless otherwise stated, scripture quotations are taken from The Holy Bible, New International Version (Anglicised edition) copyright © 1979, 1984, 2011 by Biblica. Used by permission of Hodder & Stoughton Publishers, an Hachette UK company. All rights reserved. 'NIV' is a registered trademark of Biblica. UK trademark number 1448790.

Scripture quotations taken from the Holy Bible, English Standard Version, published by HarperCollins Publishers, © 2001 Crossway Bibles, a division of Good News Publishers. Used by permission. All rights reserved.

Every effort has been made to trace and contact copyright owners for material used in this resource. We apologise for any inadvertent omissions or errors, and would ask those concerned to contact us so that full acknowledgement can be made in the future.

A catalogue record for this book is available from the British Library

Printed and bound by CPI Group (UK) Ltd, Croydon CR0 4YY

musings of a clergy child

growing into a faith of my own

Nell Goddard

Acknowledgements

This book has been born out of a 22-year journey, which I have not walked alone. So please indulge my gushing thank yous to those who have loved, cared for and encouraged me through it all.

To my publisher, The Bible Reading Fellowship, and my editor, Mike Parsons: I still can't quite believe you're letting me write this book, but thank you for all you have done throughout the process, and for believing in me enough to give me this crazy opportunity in the first place.

To the communities and churches that my parents worked in as I grew up, who loved me as one of their own, thank you: St Mary's Church, Cogges, and St James the Great, South Leigh, 1996–1999; Jesus College, Oxford, 1999–2004; Wycliffe Hall, Oxford, 1999–2008; St Andrew's Church, Oxford, 1999–2008; and Redland Parish Church, Bristol, 2008–2010.

To St James the Less Church, Pimlico, from 2010 onwards: you have taught me more about love, service, sacrifice and acceptance than I thought possible. You have shown me the value of community and modelled what it means to love till it hurts and then love some more. Thank you.

To the friends, godparents and family members who have taught me more than I dare try to put into words, loved me better than I can adequately express and encouraged me in the moments of utter despair: thank you. I could write individual paragraphs of thanks to you all, but then the acknowledgements section would be longer than the book, so you must know that this is just the tip of the iceberg: Jason and Jo Alexandre, Naomi Allen, Chris Atkinson, Eve Balshaw, Steph Buchanan, Tom Clarke, Bekah Coomber, Ben and Amabel Ealovega, Anna Edwards, Patrick and Lydia Gilday, John and Veronica Goddard, Rozzie Harrison, Ally Jones, Jerry and Stacy Kramer, Ruth and David Lockwood, Tanya Marlow, Suse McBay, Chris Morgan, Lydia Mpanga-Sebuyira, John Oliver, John and Angela Pearce, Ruth Perrin, Jane Petrie, Jennifer Schaffer-Goddard, Rick and Rachel Simpson, Josh Smedley, Amber Tallon, Alys Tarr, Jan Taylor, Kate Townsend and Nick Townsend.

To those who are not listed above because apparently even an acknowledgement page has a word limit: thank you for your friendship, your prayers, your support and your graciousness. You are so important to me; even if not acknowledged by name, please know that you have not been forgotten.

To my big brother, Jono: you have loved me deeply and protected me fiercely my whole life. Thank you for walking this journey with me, for understanding when no one else could, for being my champion co-conspirator and chief secret-keeper. There isn't anyone I would rather have done my crazy childhood alongside.

And finally, to my parents, Andrew and Lis Goddard: thank you for your unwavering obedience to God's call on our lives, for your love, support, prayers and faithfulness. But thank you most of all for never, ever failing to point me to Jesus, no matter the madness that surrounds. Mum and Dad: this one's for you.

Nell Goddard, 2017

For Mum and Dad

You gave me life, I give you this book.
This means we're even, right?

Contents

LETTERS

MUSINGS

Clergy child's lament

I didn't choose it
you called my parents to it
You made a place for me
where I thought there was none
Out of my comfort zone
and into your calling.

'Incarnational ministry,' they call it
'Invasion of personal space,' I respond
My house is not my own
my time is other people's
my life is a sermon illustration
I am to be an example to all
I apologise for things that are not my fault
I welcome in the stranger
I make small talk with anyone
'Tea or coffee? We have plenty'
is my battle cry.

I smile politely at the personal comments
about my weight
my hair
my intelligence
my family
my life.

I will share anything with them
including my parents
my dog
my sofa
my home
my life

I will share anything with them
except my mug.

I didn't choose it
you called my parents to it
You made a place for me
where I thought there was none
Out of my comfort zone
and into your calling.

To share everything
even when it hurts
To take what you have given me
every last bit of it
my parents
my dog
my sofa
my home
my life
even my mug.

To lay it at the foot of the cross
and surrender it all back
to you
Into your hands
to use as you will
to bless
to heal
to restore
to bring hope
joy
peace.

And to trust
that in all things
you will provide for me

a safe place
to hide
to cry
to scream
to rant
to question
to trust
to be angry
to be grateful
to believe.

I didn't choose it
you called my parents to it
You made a place for me
where I thought there was none
Out of my comfort zone
and into your calling.

Introduction

If you are a clergy child: welcome, friend. Kudos to you; I know how it feels: both my parents are ordained. If you're not a clergy child: welcome to you too. It's super-lovely to have you here.

This book isn't just for clergy children. If you're someone who grew up in a Christian home and therefore think that your testimony or faith story isn't particularly interesting; if you're someone who spends time questioning whether God has forgotten you in the shadow of your parents' calling; if you're uncertain whether or not you believe because you know it all with your head but you're not sure whether your heart has quite caught up yet; or if you're just a bit curious about what it's like to be a clergy child and want some fun anecdotes and amusing stories: this book's for you.

If, on the other hand, you're looking for a deep theological exegesis of ministry life, a biblical commentary, a fiction book about an imagined life in ministry, or the answers to all your questions about God, then I'm afraid you're going to have to put this book down and keep browsing. But whoever you are, whatever your story, wherever you fall on the 'ministry spectrum', or even if you don't fall on it at all, welcome.

I wrote that opening poem, 'Clergy child's lament', on a really bad day, when I was sick of feeling as if God had forgotten me in the calling of my parents, and the words of it have stuck with me ever since. And feeling forgotten is not just the case for those of us with clergy parents; if you've grown up in a Christian home, with Christian parents, going to church and praying before bed and knowing Bible stories off by heart, you can often feel a bit uninteresting. You can sometimes feel forgotten by God. Compared with friends who have remarkable conversion stories, moments of clear revelation or a miraculous healing, your 'I grew up in a Christian home and here I am, still a Christian today' testimony can feel a bit, well, boring. It can feel as if you don't really have much to offer the church, that you're not very interesting, and that God only cares about you because of who your parents are and what they do.

This isn't true.

I can't promise that this book will convince you otherwise, but I pray that as you read its words, God will speak to you about how your story is powerful because it is yours, and because he wrote it with you. I pray that his delight in you would silence the lies of comparison as you look to those people you think are 'more interesting' than you, and that instead you would grow in an understanding of your unique and precious role in God's family. I pray that as you journey through this book, however fast or slowly you read it, God will show you how much he adores you, and how he died and rose again for you. I pray that he would reveal to you that you are his beloved child, not because of who your parents are, not because of what you've done or haven't done, but because he made you and has loved you since the beginning of time.

This book is based on a blog, so it may not be set out in the way you might expect. It isn't a continuous-prose, chapter-book kind of deal, but more of a selection of short stories, tips, letters, poems and musings about life, faith, God, ministry and growing up in the church. It's the kind of book you could potentially sit down and read in one go, but I think maybe it's better just to dip in and out of it when you want to. Have a browse of the contents page, find something that seems relevant to you for the day and read that. Or use the 'Musings' section as part of your daily devotions, as a reflection on a piece of scripture or as a springboard for your own writing. This book can be used however you want, in whatever way works best for you. Plus, should you fall on hard times, I've heard that paper is edible, so you could always use it as an emergency food source.

You'll find three sections in this book: tips, letters and musings. The tips are from my blog series, 'Tips for clergy children'. They're about growing up as a clergy child, and they range from the sublime to the ridiculous. They are there primarily to (a) show you that I'm a real person, and (b) let you know that you're not alone in the madness of growing up in a Christian home. I hope they make you laugh and broaden your understanding just that little bit more of what it's like to grow up in ministry.

Next, you'll find the letters section. These are more personal, more pastoral, and they're made up of pieces of advice for particular scenarios you're most likely to come across, particularly if you're growing up in a Christian home or your parents are in ministry. They're advice from my own experience and my own story, or lessons that I've learnt because God has taught them to me at a specific time.

Finally, there are the musings. These are spiritual reflections, poems and creative writing. They're there to help you understand a little more of who God is, using my own journey as a model. They're there to remind you of those incredible truths that you've grown up being taught, to show you what a privilege it is to be growing up in a family who introduced you to God at a young age, and to inspire you to think more deeply about what your journey looks like and what you might be able to offer the church.

As a clergy child, you see, I wasn't given a choice about the life of ministry I was born into. As I've written this book, I've been asking myself: If I had the choice, would I do it again? Would I go through a childhood of being a clergy kid, a lifetime of incarnational ministry, again? Given the chance, would I have chosen this for myself? As I started writing, I didn't have the answer.

But then I found myself on a spontaneous beach trip with one of my closest friends. You could tell it was spontaneous because I was wearing skinny jeans. Everyone knows that wearing skinny jeans to the beach is a really stupid idea, because it's nigh-on impossible to roll them up for paddling in the sea. But it was warm and the sea was so inviting that I threw caution to the wind and went in anyway. I left my sandals on a rock and picked my way delicately over the pebbles towards the water's edge. Within minutes of my toes touching the cool water, I had underestimated the size of an incoming wave and the bottom of my jeans had been soaked by the sea.

I was a bit annoyed, I'll be honest with you. I had a two-hour car journey home ahead of me, and my jeans were wet. No one likes wet jeans, especially when they're skinny jeans and it's salt water that has soaked them. But then, before I could spend too long dwelling on the frustration of my damp jeans, my attention was drawn to how much I was enjoying simply paddling in the ocean. The feeling of the sand between my toes, my heels sinking into the damp ground as the waves went in and out over my feet. The cool water somehow taking the heat away from the rest of my body, because, for some reason, when your feet are cool, the rest of you is cool. It brought back memories of childhood holidays spent by the sea, swimming with my family and sunbathing with a good book. It reminded me of the time away that my family took to escape the madness of ministry— rarely outside the UK, because a clergy stipend just doesn't allow for exotic beach holidays—and how it was always an incredibly precious time for the four of us.

Despite the wet bottoms of my jeans and the long car journey home that lay ahead of me, then, I was glad I'd gone paddling. And so I realised: *I would rather have wet trousers than not to have gone in the sea at all.*

I think that's a metaphor for growing up in ministry, for being a clergy child, for learning how to grow into a faith of my own. I would rather have the inconveniences, the pain, the difficult memories, the frustrations and the scars of growing up in ministry than to not have been there at all. The joys far outweigh the trials. The laughs exceed the tears. The pleasure is ever greater than the pain. The stories of redemption speak louder than the moments of despair.

Whoever you are, wherever you find yourself in life, whatever your situation, and however wet the bottoms of your trousers are, I hope you enjoy this book. I hope and pray that it inspires you, encourages you and teaches you something of God and his love for you. I hope that you will discover just how worthwhile your wet trousers are in the light of the joy, excitement and grace you get to see and live in daily as the child of those in ministry. I hope that you will come away from this book ever more aware of the privilege it has been to grow up in a Christian home, despite the mess. But ultimately, I hope and pray that you will find in this book an encouragement to let your faith grow ever deeper as you journey with the God who has called you by name and made you his own, no matter what.

Tips for clergy children

Growing up in ministry is an experience unique to you. Your stories, your joys and your struggles will depend on your family, your location, your life and your level of involvement. They'll depend on your age, your faith and your personality. To suggest that your experience is not unique would be somewhat to misunderstand the situation.

But there are some things that are universal to those growing up in Christian homes or, more specifically, in ministry. There are some things that none of us can escape. Whether one or both of your parents are ordained, or someone in your family works part-time for the church, or you're just an active member of the congregation, there will be things you experience in ministry that you will share with thousands of others who have grown up in similar situations. It is out of these experiences that the following tips have been born.

Despite being the daughter of two ordained parents since the age of three, I only acquired the title 'clergy child' after we moved into our central London vicarage when I was 16. Although I'd spent my childhood in a Christian environment, engaging frequently in ministry, attending church and always welcoming people into our home, moving to a vicarage took the experience to a whole new level.

And so, a year in, I started compiling a list of tips for clergy children, often accompanied by an amusing anecdote or funny experience that I'd had. Being a clergy child, I guess, is kind of like 'growing up in ministry PLUS'.

As I hope you'll see from this collection of tips, growing up in ministry teaches you lessons that you won't learn anywhere else. It gives you experiences that are rare and precious, and introduces you to people you would never usually encounter. It is hard, but it is also incredible. It gives you a passion for the vulnerable that would otherwise be alien to you. It provides multiple laughs, countless ridiculous moments and a handful of life-altering encounters. It may not be easy, but it is never, ever dull, and it will form you and change you in ways that you could never even have dreamed.

This section consists of my top 20 tips, ranging from the sublime to the ridiculous. Some of them are specific to vicarage or open-home life, and some of them are just general life tips. Whatever your background, and whatever form of 'crazy' your family and home are, I hope that these tips will make you giggle and encourage you to look for the life lesson in every situation, no matter how weird it might be.

Bring-and-share lunches are highly unpredictable

There's something I think Americans have got right. Bear with me here: I'm not talking about their spelling of 'colour' or anything like that. I'm talking about bring-and-share lunches. You know what Americans call them? Potluck lunches. Previously, this had baffled me. Why would they be pot luck? Everyone brings their favourite dish, everyone gets to try everyone else's favourite dish, everyone's happy, right? Umm, not so much.

You see, when you have a church bring-and-share lunch, you not only have to specify at an early stage that food has to be brought, in order for you to be able to eat (our church notices prior to such lunches tend to consist of an announcement that 'there will be a bring-and-share lunch from 12.00 at the vicarage: please bring food/drink to share'), but it really is anyone's guess what you'll end up eating for lunch that day.

Take one Sunday in 2013, for example. We had a bring-and-share lunch to say farewell to our pastoral assistant, who was heading off to train for ordination. It was a lovely affair and she certainly got a good send-off. But it was another one of those situations where I spent a large majority of the afternoon saying, 'You just couldn't make this up,' under my breath to my dog.

As the hosts of the party, my family provided marrow provençale and gammon, with a large chocolate cake for pudding. We decided not to do any more than that because last time we had such a lunch, Mum massively overestimated the congregation's collective desire for bean salad and so we ended up eating it with every meal for the next month.

Anyway, as aforementioned, the lunch was scheduled to start at 12.00—which meant, of course, that the people started arriving at 11.20 am. We didn't let them in. You see, boundaries are excellent things, and having guests wandering around your house 40 minutes before they are invited or expected doesn't aid productivity. So we asked them to come back when the party started. And, sure enough, bang on 12 o'clock, the doorbell rang and in came the first few guests. Thankfully, they'd read the notice and had realised that they had to bring something along with them. I had the following conversation with one of the ladies who arrived first:

Lady This is a bring-and-share lunch, isn't it? That means I have to bring something, right?

Me Yup, that's right.

Lady OK, well, I brought you something.

Me Thank you, that's very kind of you. If you want to just put it on the table with the other food, that'd be great.

The lady proceeded to rummage in her bag for a little while, and then turned around and presented me with a carton of milk. Yup, one pint of milk. Considering the amount of tea we get through in our house, it was actually quite an insightful thing to bring, but maybe not your conventional bring-and-share lunch offering. The lady next to her then rummaged in her bag and handed over a bar of Cadbury Dairy Milk and some liquorice allsorts.

These two contributions set a precedent for the rest of the afternoon. Some people brought sensible things like pasta salad, roast potatoes, quiche (we are a church, after all!) or cooked chicken. Others seemed to see the lunch as an opportunity to get rid of their unwanted or expired food items. Offerings included a tin of custard, an out-of-date apple pie and 40 miniature croissants. No, really. We were about an hour in when Mum started to worry and sent someone out to get some actual vegetation. It appears to be the case that the most popular food group to bring along for such lunches is carbs.

As you might expect, we also had a fair amount of leftovers. After sending everyone home with a doggy bag of food, we packed everything else into plastic containers and stored it in the fridge-freezer. By Wednesday, we were only just halfway through the stuff, and I'd taken to offering every person who appeared in our house a defrosted miniature croissant as a snack. Unsurprisingly, not many were keen.

Sometimes the smallest offerings have the biggest impact

This tip is more of a story. It's a story of how one evening spent counting the offering at church changed my perspective on giving for ever. It's a story of generosity at its most beautiful and most heartbreaking. It's a story of the things you learn as a clergy child that you wouldn't learn anywhere else. It's a story, framed as a tip, to remind you to look for the unexpected in the ordinary and never to be afraid to have your whole worldview altered by one simple act, by someone you would never have associated with, were it not for the church.

This is a story about boiled sweets.

It was a normal Sunday, by all accounts, sometime in 2011. The 6.00 pm service at church.

> 'During the last hymn the offering will be taken. If you are a visitor at this church, please do not feel under any obligation to give. This is very much for our church family. Anything given will be used to further the work of the church here in the parish and further afield.'

The same words every week.

As a member of the PCC, it was my job—along with the verger—to count the collection at the end of the service. As usual, we tipped the offering bag upside down and let the coins, notes and envelopes fall on to the desk. A quick shake of the bag, and we began counting.

Except that this week there was something different.

In among all the shiny coins and slightly crumpled notes, there lay a solitary boiled sweet—a reddish colour, wrapped in crispy, crinkly cellophane.

I'll be honest, I laughed it off. I brushed it aside as a joke, an accident, a moment of madness by one of our more 'interesting' parishioners. Chuckling to myself, I left the sweet to one side and finished counting the money. I can't even remember what the total came to. In jest, we noted the addition of the boiled sweet at the bottom of the collection sheet.

Later that evening, sitting at home having post-church dinner with my mum, I mentioned the boiled sweet. I recounted it as a funny story, a 'look how wacky our church is!' tale to wheel out at dinner parties.

But then my mum stopped me.

'Yes,' she said quietly, 'I know about that. One of the ladies came up to me at the end of the service this evening. She said she hoped I wouldn't mind, but she put a boiled sweet in the offering. Her benefits ran out on Friday and she hasn't been able to afford food for the weekend, so she's been living on boiled sweets. When she heard that the offering would be used to help the work of the parish, she knew she didn't have any money, so she decided that she would give up her final boiled sweet instead.'

Wow.

In that moment, I nearly cried. Suddenly, the widow's mite (Mark 12:41–44; Luke 21:1–4) became a reality. 'These people gave their gifts out of their wealth,' Jesus said, 'but she out of her poverty put in all she had to live on.' Suddenly, the direct debit of however much per month I give to the church felt like a pittance compared with the generosity of this woman. The humble gift of one without enough to eat, who gives to the church what, realistically, cannot make a difference to its work, is 1000 times more than I have ever considered giving.

There are so many lessons to be learnt from this simple story. When you understand that sometimes the smallest offerings have the biggest impact, you learn something of what it means to truly give of yourself. You realise how much we, the church, could learn from those who have very little, if only we were to pay slightly more attention. You learn how important it is to be a part of a church that welcomes in the rich and the poor with open arms, that doesn't discriminate and places the vulnerable at the very centre of their community. But I think the thing I learned most of all from this story is that the size or scale of the gift doesn't matter; what matters is the attitude with which it is given. And sometimes, I have learnt, the smallest gifts have the biggest impact.

People will come in and randomly start dismantling your house

'An Englishman's home is his castle'—a well-known saying which contains within it all the unspoken rules about what you don't do in other people's houses—draw on walls, invade without express permission, comment loudly on the distasteful decor... you know the drill. A vicar's vicarage, however, is not a castle. A vicar's vicarage is a hotel/B&B/restaurant/luggage drop-off point/library/place to practise your DIY skills and numerous other things. This is exacerbated exponentially if you operate an open-home policy, as my family does, thus creating some interesting scenarios.

Take 2010, for example. We'd been living in our house for a few months and everything was going well. Our thighs were beginning to get used to all the stairs; we'd come to know which doors banged and which floorboards creaked. Everything was running smoothly. Other members of the church, however, appeared to feel differently, especially about one particular thing. The main door leading out of our kitchen was set on a spring. This meant that it automatically closed with quite a loud bang whenever you left it open. Annoying, but useful for keeping our intensely inquisitive dog out of the recycling and preventing her from greeting guests at the front door.

Just a few weeks earlier, we had started a women's prayer meeting on Wednesday mornings at our house. This meant that trays of tea and coffee had to be carried from the kitchen to the upstairs sitting room at 7.00 am, and back again at 8.15 am.

Now, we would usually just prop the downstairs door open with a chair if we knew we would be coming back with our hands full and be unable to open the door. But for one of the lovely ladies at the prayer meeting, this was a step too far. When she arrived downstairs with a tray, and the door was closed, she became frustrated and decided to take matters into her own hands. She put down the tray and made her way to the toolbox in the downstairs sitting room. From it she grabbed a hammer, some pliers and a screwdriver. She walked swiftly back to the kitchen door and, before any of us had realised what was happening, she had undone the screws attaching the doorspring to the door and removed part of the metal.

We finally realised what she was doing when, with a loud BANG, the spring came undone. By that time, of course, it was too late to stop it. With a victorious 'Aha!' the lady removed the spring from the inside of the door and proceeded to demonstrate how the door would now stay open all by itself. Useful in some aspects, but, as the spring was technically also a fire-safety measure, possibly not the most sensible of things to do—especially without first seeking permission.

This was probably my first real experience of 'crazy things that happen in a vicarage' and it set a good precedent for all that was to come over the next few years.

So, an Englishman's home is his castle. And a vicar's vicarage? Well, that's for you to decide.

Do not give out your address over the phone

We get a lot of phone calls in our house. It's just a fact of life in a vicarage, I think. It has its advantages: there's almost always someone to talk to if you fancy a chat, and, if you don't like silence, you never get too uncomfortable. There are, however, a number of disadvantages as well. For example, people seem to forget that phones will not magically identify them (unless caller ID is in place), so they frequently fail to realise that the person answering the phone is unlikely to recognise who the caller is, even though the caller recognises them. This is important to remember: just because the caller knows who they're talking to, it doesn't mean you have to be embarrassed to ask who they are. After all, they had a pool of maybe four potential people to choose from. You have a pool of 400 callers, if not more.

The identification process is important to remember when answering the phone in a vicarage, especially because people will sometimes (I mean, often) ask for personal details. Just because they talk to you politely and as if they know you, it does not mean you have to give them whatever they ask for by way of information. No, really, you don't.

Back in 2012, I got a phone call from a friendly sounding old man. After checking that he had called the correct household, he asked for my postal address, as he wanted to send my father something. I have to admit that I was about to tell him when I realised I had absolutely no idea who I was speaking to. So I asked him, 'Who's speaking, please?' The response was quite unusual: 'I'm sorry, this is a private matter; I just want to send a parcel to the doctor' (my dad has a PhD). At this point I decided to run up seven flights of stairs in order to give the phone to my dad.

It seems obvious not to give out personal details on the phone, but when you're hearing the friendly voice of someone who seems to know you of old, common sense often takes a back seat. So, just remember—ask the caller to identify themselves, and, if they refuse to do so, don't give them any information. Let's be honest, if you're a vicar's child or, indeed, if you're a member of a church, you probably have enough 'interesting' people in your life already, without adding anyone else to the list through an inability to keep a hold on your personal details. Trust me, seeming rude is a price worth paying to ensure that fewer people know your address.

Boundaries are excellent things

Boundaries. For some, this word suggests a terrifying concept. For others, it is a godsend. Initially, I fell into the former category. Why would I have boundaries? Someone might need me! But then, when we moved into the vicarage, I began to learn the true value of boundaries. They are beautiful, beautiful things.

As a vicar, or a member of a vicar's family, especially if you operate an open home, you are considered public property. Don't get me wrong; this is a lovely thing in most situations. Having the ability to share your home with people who might not have one in which they are comfortable, or the means to show love to people by giving them cups of tea and feeding them cake is incomparable. It is truly fabulous a great deal of the time. But there have to be limits.

My mother introduced me to a brilliant word the other day. She said I was allowed to use it any time I wanted, to anyone I wanted, when they asked me to do something for them. It's very short, but highly effective; only one syllable, but it can save you a great deal of time, argument and awkwardness. It goes something like this: 'No'.

And I can actually use it. When someone comes to my house in the middle of the afternoon when I'm home alone and asks for a cup of tea, I can say 'No'. When someone outstays their welcome in my house and I just want to go to bed, I can say 'No' to their next request and then ask them to leave. *And it actually works.*

I spent a long time being terrified of offending people, because they needed me or because I felt guilty for refusing when they'd asked so nicely. But I'm beginning to learn the many benefits of saying 'No'. It means that you're not forced into having company when you'd much rather be alone. It means you can have a quiet evening in if you want to. It means you can get on with the really exciting part in your book before you go to sleep, because the people you invited round didn't outstay their welcome.

So, my friends, embrace your boundaries. They will serve you well. You honour them, and they will honour you. Just practise using the word 'No'. I promise, it will come in useful at least five times a week.

Don't feel obliged to invite the entire congregation to your birthday party

Do you remember the stress of trying to put together a birthday party guest list as a child? My parents always imposed a twelve-friend limit on our birthday parties (reasonable when you're on a small clergy stipend and don't have a garden), but it was always so stressful trying to pick our favourite friends while also attempting not to offend anyone. Somehow, I managed it successfully every year and made it through primary school unscathed.

I thought I was done with birthday party invitation list politics when I reached my tenth birthday and the twelve-friend limit was lifted. How wrong I was! When my mum got her first incumbency, I realised that the politics of being a vicar's child can extend even to one's birthday parties. (For those of you not down with the Church of England lingo, an incumbency is a posh title for being a vicar of a parish.)

The thing is, church politics are hard to negotiate, and as a clergy child you can often feel under pressure not to offend anyone in the congregation at any time. As a human being, however, you will be very much aware that this is impossible. Also, just a little bonus tip for you: it's not your responsibility to keep everyone in the church congregation happy. I know you probably don't believe me, but it is actually true.

Anyway, back to birthday parties. It was about seven months after we'd moved into the vicarage, and I was planning my 17th birthday party. I had invited some school friends, some friends from the place where we used to live and a couple of people from church who I got on with especially well. But then it hit me, in a classic bout of teenage-induced angst: people talk. If I invited this person from church, surely it meant I had to invite that person. And if I invited that person, then

I had to invite this other person. I scrawled a few more names down on the list. Then a few more. And in the end, before I knew it, I had written on my list the entire church congregation—all 50 of them.

Later that day, I sidled up to my mum and together we tried to work out a solution. Despite her reassurances that I really didn't need to invite all these people to my birthday party, and they really, truly, honestly wouldn't be offended if they found out they weren't invited, my fear of offending people won out. Finally, my mum and I reached a compromise: I would have one party for my close friends (a murder-mystery party, so I had an explanation for not inviting everyone) and another party, another day, for everyone else. That way, no one would feel left out, and I wouldn't end up accidentally offending anyone.

My birthday came around, and both parties were great. I mean, who doesn't love having two birthday parties? Also, they were both fancy dress, which was obviously completely excellent. But, if I'm really honest, I learnt a lesson from the second birthday party: if you only invite people because you're worried you'll offend them if you don't, rather than just inviting your close friends, the event will probably end up feeling more like a duty than a joy. Don't get me wrong: I had fun, and I grew closer to a number of people I hadn't really known beforehand, but I did spend most of the time feeling like the vicar's daughter rather than me in my own right. Realistically, that's not what you want at your birthday party. A birthday party should feel like a birthday party rather than a church function.

So, friends, a tip for you: no matter how much of an obligation you feel to invite everyone in the church to your birthday party, out of fear that you might offend them, don't. You are a human being, and there will be some people in the church who you get on with better than others. That is OK. Your birthday party is your birthday party; it is not an opportunity or an obligation to make everyone like you or to keep everyone else happy. There are some situations where it is wise, as a clergy child, to be open to issuing general invitations, but your birthday party is not one of them. Sometimes, it's OK to be picky.

You will never realise how important your hospitality is until you're on the receiving end of someone else's

Back in 2013, I went on a gap year trip with a group to Zanzibar for eleven weeks. It was an incredible trip as we worked in local communities as well as helping with the local church. My time there changed a lot of things for me. One of the many things I learned while I was away was the importance of hospitality, and what it is like to be on the receiving end of hospitality instead of being the one offering it. It was a humbling and eye-opening experience.

On our first full day, we went to visit a family who lived about a ten-minute bus ride away from our house. They were lovely, really welcoming and informative—all the things you would expect from a family working for the church. The first time we were at their house, they told us, 'You're always welcome here, any time.' Great, lovely, thanks. 'We'll bear that in mind,' we said. Because, you know, when people in England say that, what they really mean is, 'You're welcome here as long as you give me at least two days' warning and don't stay for more than an hour, because otherwise you'll ruin my schedule for the day, eat all my food and bore me witless.'

But this family actually did mean it. They meant it in a way that almost all the group members found really hard to understand.

For the first few weeks, we worried about 'overstaying our welcome', 'intruding' and 'being a burden', until we realised that the family really wanted us there. They enjoyed it. They loved the fact that, by week six, we would just walk into their house without knocking and head straight to the kitchen to grab a drink, sit down and use their internet. They wanted us to feel at home in their home.

For us, for the team, this was such a gift. In a strange, hot country, where not many people speak your language and the culture is completely different, a place to relax, eat home-cooked food, use the internet and take full advantage of the air conditioning was a godsend. It was a home away from home. And more than just opening their home to us, the family opened their hearts as well. They became our family. Saying goodbye to them was like saying goodbye to a second set of parents. They laughed with us, cried with us, prayed with us, loved us, fed us, watered us, filled us up with delicious cookies, let us use their oven to bake birthday cakes, ferried us around in their car, took us to the doctor when we were ill, let us invite other friends over (at one point there were 14 teenagers sitting in their house eating chicken and pizza) and simply loved us as their own children. It was amazing.

While I was sitting in their home, looking round their sitting room filled with teenagers and laughter, the boys staring at the Xbox screen open mouthed as they played FIFA, and being grateful for what a gift God had given us in this family, I realised that, actually, this is exactly what my family does in England. This is what we offer to people in London who don't have anywhere else to call home. All this love, being welcomed into a family when your family is miles away and you sometimes feel so alone that it's scary—this unconditional, unlimited love and food and cups of tea and 'What's mine is yours; no, really'—this is what being a Christian family, a vicar's family, is all about. It's about sharing what you have that others need. It's about opening your arms, your home and your heart to anyone and everyone, no matter how hard you might find it. No matter how much you might want the doorbell not to ring when you're about to settle down with your mum to watch a film, and for someone not to traipse in needing a cup of tea and some love. No matter how much you wish you could go downstairs in your pyjamas once in a while, because getting dressed first thing in the morning is so much effort. No matter what, this is what we are called to do. And you will never realise the value of it until you are on the receiving end.

So, next time you wish that your house was your own and that everyone else would just go away and leave you alone, put on a smile, offer them a cup of tea and welcome them in, because you never know what a blessing you might be to them in that moment. You see, when Jesus said, 'Love your neighbour as yourself' (Mark 12:30), he was making quite a good point.

Always lock the toilet door. A surprising number of people will just barge through closed ones

This is a lesson for all people everywhere—a public service announcement, if you will. It does, however, apply particularly in a vicarage, as you have an above-average number of people using your house (and toilet) on a day-to-day basis.

A while back, our downstairs toilet door lock broke. For most people, this would be a mild inconvenience. For us, it was a full-blown disaster, because the downstairs toilet is the 'public' toilet in our house. But, as it turned out, this was actually a learning opportunity *disguised* as a disaster.

You see, it was through this disaster that I discovered just how many people will happily walk straight into the toilet, even when the door is closed. You would be surprised at how many it is. (I think my record was six in one week.) This means that when you are on the toilet, you not only have to concentrate on weeing, but you also have to keep an ear out for anyone approaching the door, and then be ready to shout out 'I'm in here!' or 'BACK OFF RIGHT NOW!' as they reach for the handle, about to expose to the world the fact that you enjoy reading *The Week* while on the toilet.

So, the lesson from this tip is to lock the toilet door. More than that, when your parent says, 'Oh, I'll fix the lock when I have time,' do not believe them. They will *never* have time. Just get out a screwdriver and do it yourself, or face the embarrassment of having to make small talk at church with someone who walked in on you weeing 24 hours earlier. Trust me, it's worth learning how to use a screwdriver just to avoid having to do that.

Teach your parent to turn off their phone

To some people, this would seem like a bit of a non-tip, as surely every adult must know how to turn off their mobile phone. Well, my friends, prepare to have your preconceptions challenged. This is not the case.

My mother, bless her, is one of those people who 'puts up with' technology, by which I mean she copes. She muddles on through. It seems that she and technology have a mutual agreement not to annoy each other and then they get on just fine. They both go about their day-to-day business, using each other as they see fit. This seems, for the most part, to work pretty well.

When my mother got a smartphone, however, this all changed. Suddenly, technology was available 24/7. Emails were there to be read, texts were needing replies and phone calls were having to be answered. My father, being the wise man that he is, foresaw this problem and therefore, when setting up her phone for her, he scheduled it to turn off automatically between the hours of 11.00 pm and 7.00 am. He did this unbeknown to my mother, who for some reason didn't notice the fact that her phone would never go off during the night.

Fast-forward a few months, and one evening at 10.00 pm my mum asks me to type out an email for her on her phone, because I'm faster at typing than she is (sign of a misspent youth, she says). So she dictates and I duly type. I then send the message and turn off her phone for her. I inform her of this action, and the following conversation ensues:

Me   OK, done. And I've turned off your phone.

Mum   What? You turned off my phone? How?

Me   Well, I pressed and held the big red button with the power symbol next to it until the phone went off.

Mum Seriously? I did not know you could do that!

Me   What, you mean you never turn off your phone? What about in church?

Mum Oh, I just put it on silent… I didn't know you could actually turn it off. That's amazing!

There you have it. Not every adult knows how to turn off their phone, but every adult can learn, and it is a valuable lesson. So, my technology-literate friends, do check that your parent knows how to turn off their phone—you might be surprised by the answer.

Make sure you check out the parish profile before your parent applies for a job

Back in 2010, my mother started looking for an incumbency. Searching for an incumbency usually involves getting *The Church of England Newspaper* or *The Church Times* and looking at their Vacancies page (towards the back). If you see a church you like the look of, you go on to its website and download its parish profile. A parish profile is like a lonely hearts ad for a church. You know: 'One London church WLTM ordained minister, 20+, looking for LTR, holy, likes people, visionary, GSOH, passionate about Jesus.' OK, possibly slightly more coherent, but that's the gist of it.

Anyway, my parents operate an excellent system in that everyone in the family is involved in each step of the decision-making process when they are applying for jobs. This means that we talk before they start looking, and then they send us parish profiles to read and give feedback on. They'll only apply for jobs that we're happy about. My brother and I have always really valued this system (sneaky tip for vicars with children: do this; it'll pay off).

The issue I faced with the churches my mother was considering was that they all looked really interesting, and the description of the ideal incumbent always almost perfectly matched her. This is because my mother is one of those people who was born to be a vicar—it is so completely and utterly her. It's not a job, it's a vocation, and she's brilliant at it. If you met her, you would see what I mean. This did, however, leave me with a problem: she could apply for all these jobs and would probably be shortlisted for all of them (unless they didn't want a woman, in which case she was likely to struggle somewhat).

So, instead of looking at what the church wanted, I decided to look at what I wanted—the vicarage. The importance of this is not to be underestimated. Every incumbency comes with a vicarage. Vicarages have to have certain things in them: at least four bedrooms, a decent kitchen and at least two reception rooms. Not too shabby, eh? Well, I decided that I would only 'OK' parishes with vicarages that lived up to my standards. So when my mother sent me parish profiles, I would skim-read the main bit and scroll to the last page to check out the vicarage. Some of them were fabulous. Eight bedrooms? Yes, please! Some, on the other hand, were not so good. Bungalow? Uh, no thanks.

There are many things that a vicar requires for their house, and these priorities are all well and good, but what about the vicar's children's requirements? Below are my top three things to look out for when auditioning a vicarage for potential liveability. I've made the list so that you don't have to. You are welcome.

- A clear divide between 'family space' and 'public space'. Whether it's a door, a staircase or just a polite notice, make sure there's an obvious dividing line between where parishioners are allowed and where family can go. This means that there is always somewhere to escape to when the sheer number of people in your house gets overwhelming. Whether you think so or not, this will happen.
- A separation between the family sitting room and the 'parishioner meeting room'. In some vicarages, your parent might have a big enough study to meet parishioners in there. Great. But in some, they will not. If that is the case, make sure there is another area in the house where they can meet, which is not the family relaxing space. Vicars tend to have a lot of evening meetings, and the last thing you want is for a PCC meeting to be happening in the room with the TV when *The Great British Bake Off* is on.
- Proximity to the church. This is an interesting one, as vicarages are often right next door to the church but can sometimes be a few streets away. I can't tell you which is best for you, but make sure you take into consideration a few factors. The closer your house is to the church, the less time it will take you to get to church on Sundays, the easier it will be to escape at the end of a service, and

the closer you will be to your parent's work space should there be an emergency. On the other hand, if it's very nearby, everyone will know it's the vicarage. This is sometimes a good thing: your friends will never get lost finding your house, the postman will never deliver your post to the wrong place (if it's addressed correctly) and so on. But it can also be a bit of a pain, as more people will come knocking and asking for stuff if they know it's a vicarage, and everyone in the church will know where to find you, night or day.

So remember—check out the vicarage. If you're going to have to live there, and especially if you're going to have hundreds of people in and out each week, you definitely have to make sure there will be enough room not only for them but also for you. And, most importantly of all, make sure there is room in your bedroom for people to come and stay—because, trust me, sometimes you'll need old, sane friends to visit, just to remind you what normality is like.

Learn to accept strange gifts with grace

Everyone knows the feeling you get at Christmas, or on your birthday, when you open that one present that, well, you don't really know what to do with. Maybe it's a pair of lime-green socks from your rather unusual uncle, or a piece of jewellery from your second cousin three times removed, who has suddenly decided that you desperately need this family heirloom in your life. Whatever it is, we all know that the polite thing to do is to smile nicely and try to thank your relative as sincerely as you can.

Thankfully, for most people, these kinds of occurrences happen only with slightly eccentric family members, once or twice a year. Or maybe three times, if the one crazy relative that everyone has comes to visit and brings bags of presents for you. But anyway, it doesn't happen very often. The thing is, though, when you live in a vicarage it could happen most weeks. One of my vicarage-dwelling friends once messaged me to share her story of finding a heavy ceramic statuette of a rabbit washing a baby rabbit left on the doorstep, with no note attached.

From the large red plastic brooch pressed into my hand one Sunday evening to the bright-green string vest proudly presented to me one Saturday afternoon, random gifts are never far off. But my favourite random-gift-from-a-parishioner story actually happened to my dad a few Christmases ago.

8.00 pm, Christmas Day. Everyone has left (after all, Christmas is never 'just family time'), and we're settling down to watch some Christmas TV together as a family. Then the doorbell goes. Confused, my mum gets up to answer it and, a few minutes later, we hear two pairs of footsteps coming inside. It's someone who was invited for Christmas lunch but didn't quite make it on time. So we feed him some leftovers and make polite Christmassy conversation while he eats. A couple of hours later, Mum's exhausted. She heads up to bed and I follow, leaving Dad downstairs to show the guest out. Dad manages to get him to the doorstep, when suddenly the visitor stops. The following conversation occurs:

Him   Thank you for dinner. I have a present for you, actually.

Dad   Oh, thank you very much, that's very kind of you. You really don't have to do that.

Him   No, I want you to have them. I hope you like them. Happy Christmas.

The gentleman proceeds to rummage in one of the many carrier bags he's holding, then pulls out a single white pair of Calvin Klein underpants and hands them solemnly to my dad. When my dad (understandably) looks baffled, he tells him not to worry because 'they're clean and new, I promise'. Dad, in the excellent clergy way that he has, thanks the gentleman kindly, wishes him a happy Christmas and shuts the door.

Mum's response? 'Well, at least he gave them to *you*. It would have been even weirder if he'd presented me with underwear on the doorstep!' A valid point, but possibly not what my dad wanted to hear at that point in time.

So, next time you open that random gift from your great-uncle that you don't know what to do with, be grateful it's not a pair of underpants presented to you on your doorstep by a parishioner. And practise smiling and saying 'thank you' nicely—it'll come in handy in a great number of situations, I promise.

You are, to all intents and purposes, the vicarage social secretary

Vicars are busy people. Don't let anyone tell you otherwise. Vicars are often also highly sociable people, especially if they are extroverts. This means that vicars like to have people around a lot. As they are overwhelmingly busy, however, visits often fail to get arranged with a definite date. My mother, for example, is the wonderful kind of person who is so hospitable that she will tell people to 'come and stay whenever' or 'pop round for a cup of tea at some point' and actually expect them to take it literally. She seems to forget that we are British, and therefore everything must be organised and timed correctly.

As she is so very busy, she often forgets to reply to emails asking whether 'X' can come and stay the night or come round for dinner. This presents a problem, because the person has been assured that they can 'pop round whenever', but social convention dictates that they must arrange a convenient time slot to make an appearance. They are, it would seem, stuck between a rock and a hard place. That's where the vicar's child comes in. As a vicar's child, you are your parent's social calendar. You are pretty much in charge of all social gatherings that have the potential to happen at your house. You are responsible for making sure that:

- not too many people are there all at once.
- people who harbour a barely concealed loathing for each other are never invited for dinner at the same time.
- your parent is aware of who is coming for dinner, when they are arriving and how long they are expecting to stay.
- your parent is briefed on the names of the people coming for dinner or to stay the night.
- your parent does not accidentally book in a meeting for the time when someone's coming to eat, drink tea or stay the night.

As I'm sure you're aware, vicars have the very best of intentions, especially when it comes to replying to all correspondence. But often it happens that they receive an email, make a note in their head of what to say in response, and then assume that their reply has been sent by telepathy to the person concerned, thus failing to tell them anything. It happens to the best of us, but, it seems, particularly to those who are ordained.

I would therefore recommend that, as a clergy child, you tell everyone to whom your parent issues general invitations that if they wish to get a reply about when they should arrive, when they should leave, what they should bring and so on, they should get in contact with you. You not only have more time than your parent but you can also get a verbal response from them and write the visitor an email, rather than relying on the somewhat flaky mode of telepathy in which vicars seem to invariably put their trust.

If someone's coming to stay, make sure you're informed well in advance

As I've mentioned, a key part of my family's ministry is what we call an 'open home'. This means that people can come and go as they like, and we'll never stop anyone coming to stay. Being an introvert who is perfectly happy with her own company and occasionally finds other people overwhelming, I have been known to struggle with this policy, but my brother, who is a people person to the max, relishes the opportunity to invite friends to stay. He enjoys it so much, in fact, that he frequently invites them to come and stay even when he's not around. There was a time, a few years back, when these guests were usually people only he knew—so we repeatedly had strangers staying in our house, with my brother nowhere to be seen.

Now, life is busy and sometimes things slip our minds. Sometimes these things matter; sometimes they do not. Sometimes my brother remembered to tell us that people were staying; sometimes he did not. Sometimes he told my parents and they remembered; sometimes he told them and they promptly forgot.

Exhibit A: the 2012 Olympics. London was packed and accommodation was scarce. My brother had a friend working at the Olympics who needed a place to stay in London. He offered, and the friend accepted. The friend wasn't going to get back from work until late evening, so my brother kindly lent him his house keys. All very well, except that no one thought to tell me.

Cue one sleepy, summery Thursday night. Mum and I have taken the dog around the block for the last time and she's gone to bed. Dad and brother are away. I settle down to watch *Mock the Week*. It's about 10.20 pm when I think I hear the front door open quietly and then close again. I mute the TV and listen carefully. Nothing. So I carry on watching. Next thing I know, I hear someone coming slowly downstairs. My heart starts to race. I shout, 'Hello? Mum?' in the hope that it's just my mother wanting a glass of water. No response. I hear the sitting-room door open and my palms begin to sweat. More footsteps. I say again, 'Mum?' No answer. Then suddenly a figure appears around the corner. I scream and jump about a foot in the air. My dog, being the brilliant guard dog that she is, immediately jumps up and runs to the intruder, wagging her tail and demanding to be greeted.

Thankfully, it was just my brother's friend, who is very nice and non-threatening. He was also highly apologetic for giving me a small heart attack. Even so, I've learnt my lesson. Now, every evening before my parents go to bed, I check with them: no one's arriving to stay tonight, are they? For the sake of your blood pressure, I recommend you do the same.

It's okay to grieve

I had five missed calls from my mum. It's the universal signal that something is not quite right. I rang her back but she said she couldn't talk, as she was on her way to a meeting and didn't want to tell me over the phone without enough time to explain properly. That worried me. I headed home to find my dad standing outside our house. 'What's happened?' I questioned, bad situations and worst-case scenarios racing through my head. With his voice breaking and tears in his eyes, he told me. Mark, one of our parishioners, had died.

I don't think I'll ever forget it. It was such a strange mix of emotions, some that I couldn't really name and still struggle with now. The death of someone in your church family does that to you, you see. It inspires within you such a host of thoughts and feelings that it's nigh on impossible to pull them apart and put labels on them. These people are not blood relatives and you would probably never have associated with them, or even met them, were it not for the church. Yet you've spent so much time with them and know so much of their story that it feels wrong to call them anything but family—brothers and sisters in Christ.

Fast-forward a few weeks—time for the funeral. It was a deeply emotional day, as my mum led the service and my dad preached, both of them fighting back tears throughout. It was only the second funeral I'd ever attended and I didn't really know how to deal with it, so, the day after, I headed right back up to university, determined to continue with my degree and try not to think about all the emotions running through my head and battering at my heart.

Eight months later, it was Christmas. I didn't expect it to be difficult. I know how to do Christmas. Christmas is a time for celebration and joy, feasting and laughter. But Mark, you see, had spent every

Christmas with us since we'd arrived in London. Ever since 2010, we'd opened our home to those who would otherwise be spending Christmas on their own. It resulted in having a very eclectic bunch of people around the table. They were mostly different every year, but there were always a few who never failed to show up. Mark was one of them. By 2014, my brother and I had spent more Christmases with him than we had with our own grandparents.

In 2015, however, Mark was missing. Having Christmas lunch without him was a strange experience. He wasn't always an easy person to be around, and it is important not to sugarcoat the times of frustration and difficulty, but Christmas with him—and with all those who join us—was and is always a joy.

We raised a glass to him over Christmas lunch that year, just as the chocolate pudding (the bit he looked forward to all year, he told us annually) came to the table. It sparked in me a strange feeling of joy mixed with grief—grief as we missed spending Christmas with a friend and a brother, but joy because we do not 'grieve as others do who have no hope' (1 Thessalonians 4:13, ESV), and we live in the knowledge that he is with God.

Days later, I found a method of grieving. It didn't involve tears, raging, swearing or shouting. It involved writing. I'm not able to give you tips on how to cope with death, because it looks different for each person and with each loss. But what I can do is encourage you to grieve however you see best, in whatever way is healthy for you. Whether it's by crying or writing or painting or dancing or singing or reading or walking, please learn to grieve. The sad fact is that when you live in a vicarage or grow up in ministry, you see a lot of pain and you may experience death first-hand more often than your friends. So learn how to grieve—alone and in community, with other people and by yourself. Process emotions, grieve and give your sorrow back to God in the knowledge that he weeps with those who weep, and is the great comforter.

I must end this tip with the piece that I wrote in honour of Mark, to show you how grief comes at the most unexpected times and in the strangest of ways. I publish it here in memory of those we have loved and lost in our church families and as a declaration of hope, because, as those who believe in the risen saviour, we know that death is never the end.

To an absent friend

Five Christmases we'd spent
with you in our lives.
This year it was different
but that's no surprise.

We had guests a-plenty
for lunch, as we do,
but your life was remembered
and your presence missed, too.

Many years we'd feasted,
sat all around.
Some years you spoke,
some not making a sound.

It wasn't always easy,
you weren't always fun,
but we'd rather have you at all
than have you at none.

It was strange not to hear
your exclamation of joy:
'The best bit of the year!'
you'd grin like a boy.

Chocolate pudding with sauce—
'twas as simple as that—
passed down the table
to where you were sat.

And so, this is us:
a mismatched bunch
of strangers and friends
in the middle of lunch.

Then we all raise our glasses.
'To an absent friend,' we cry.
It's odd you're not here,
there's a tear in our eye.

Happy Christmas, dear Mark,
a greatly missed friend—
but home now with Jesus;
for death's not the end.

In memory of Mark Nelson,
23 February 1972—8 April 2015

Don't bother waiting for your parents before leaving church. It's a waste of everyone's time

This tip is something that I learnt very early on, as a child, even when my parents weren't running a church. When you've been in a church for a long time, you see, you know a lot of people. And when you know a lot of people, a lot of people want to talk to you. This is fine if you're the one being talked to. People are interesting and conversations are fun. It is less fine, however, if you are not the one being talked to, but are in the care of the one being talked to—especially if you are unable to leave until the one being talked to has stopped being talked to.

When I was a child, we lived a solid 20 minutes' walk from church. This meant there was no chance of a swift exit after the service, no option to steal the house keys and wander home safely. No, I had to stay. This was problematic for me, as a seven-year-old, when my parents decided to converse with people for at least 45 minutes after church every week. When you're a vicar's child (or, indeed, the child of anyone who is well known and loved in the church), you have to promote the view that you are well-mannered and polite, which means that you cannot grab your parent's hand and start walking while they're still talking. (I tried that once. It didn't work.) It got to the point where I would go and find the church book collection, settle down with a slightly-too-old-for-me theological exploration of something or other, and read until my parents came to find me.

When I was old enough to have house keys, however, a whole new realm of freedom was discovered: I could walk home unsupervised. When I wanted. How I wanted. With whom I wanted. It was seriously exciting. The service would finish and I had the choice just to walk home. I was still, however, young and naive, and was therefore often convinced by my mother's declaration that she would 'only be a little while'. Because of this, I often ended up waiting for her all the same. Once, I was informed by my mother that she would be 'under five minutes'. Half an hour later, I was still there.

This failure of parents to leave church never ceases to amaze me. Even now, aged 22, I still fall for it. 'I'll only be five minutes!' they say. 'I'd love to walk home with you and chat!' they plead. And there I am, half an hour later, longing for a cup of tea and a cuddle with my dog.

So, my friends, don't wait for your parents to leave church. It will only end in frustration and wasted time. Trust me; I know.

There are certain things you should never tell a caller

Phone calls are a minefield. It's so easy to blurt out the strangest things without any thought for the consequences. Particularly as a clergy child, however, there are certain types of information you should never give to a caller who has asked to speak to one of your parents. I have learnt this the hard way, but I hope that by providing you with my list of no-go suggestions, I can save you from any future embarrassment. So here are my top ten.

1 Never tell a caller that your parent is on the toilet. Neither the caller nor your parents appreciate having this information shared. In addition, never qualify the statement with '… but they'll call you back in 15 minutes'. Just because your parent likes to read on the toilet, it does not mean that the caller needs to know.

2 Never tell the caller that you have no idea who they are, once they've introduced themselves. At least pretend to know them until you can pass the phone to your parent.

3 Never scowl when answering the phone. They know.

4 Never sigh loudly when the person says who's calling. They take it personally.

5 If you need to shout to your parent that someone is calling for them, remember to cover the mouthpiece, or you'll deafen the poor soul on the other end of the line.

6 Even if you're using caller ID, never, ever answer the phone with 'Hello, [name]', because you'll probably have got the wrong person. This happened to my brother once. The caller ID said 'Paul' so he assumed it was our uncle. He answered with a bright 'Hello, Uncle Paul!' and ended up having an exceptionally awkward conversation with a nice man called Paul who was not our uncle and couldn't understand why my brother thought he was.

7 Before you pick up the phone, find out whether or not your parent is 'busy'. Never let the caller hear you say, 'It's X; are you busy?' because they will assume that your parent's availability is dependent on who the caller is. Even though this might be the case, the caller does not need to know it.

8 Never say that your parent will definitely call the person back. Always use a qualifier (for example, if they've finished their sermon, if they're not too busy, if I remember to tell them you called…).

9 Never ask a caller why they are calling 'again'. This is not polite.

10 Never talk to a caller about something that they personally have not told you about—otherwise they'll know that you overheard that conversation between your parents and get really annoyed.

Always carry ID. You never know when you might need to prove yourself

Back in 2014 I learnt a valuable life lesson. As a 19-year-old who didn't buy alcohol or 18-rated films very often, I didn't use my ID much at all. In fact, I once almost removed it from my wallet, because I like to have only one card per slot and I was running out of slots. (Don't judge me; I know I'm weird.) But, thankfully, I kept it in.

'But why?' I hear you ask. It was not because I had decided to go crazy and buy lots of alcohol and 18-rated films (maybe another day…). It was, in fact, because I went to church.

No, really. One Wednesday morning, I headed off to church to help our lovely administrator with a bit of paperwork. As it happened, I arrived before the administrator and, not having had the presence of mind to take some church keys, I had to wait outside. I dutifully hovered, minding my own business, until an old, vaguely unkempt man approached me. Our conversation went something like this:

Him You. Do you work here?

Me No. Why?

Him I'm looking for the person in charge. I want to talk to the person in charge. I want to ask about the church's music licence. I want to talk to the person in charge. Where are they?

Me I'm afraid they're not here at the moment. The administrator is on his way; he should be here shortly.

Him No. I don't want to talk to the administrator. I want to talk to the person in charge. I want to talk to these people. *(Pointing to the poster advertising the Sunday services, with my parents' names on it.)* Where are they? When will they be here?

Me   Oh, those are my parents. I don't know when my mum will be here, though.

Him   *(Looking at me suspiciously.)* They're your parents? Really?

Me   Yes, really.

Him   Can I see some ID, please?

Me   Umm, sorry, what?

Him   Some identification. Anyone could claim to be their daughter. You need to prove that you really are.

So I got out my provisional driving licence and showed him that, yes, I really was who I claimed to be. Not that it would have made much difference if I wasn't. I mean, what thing of worth could I possibly have done while moonlighting as a clergy child? Recited the communion liturgy off by heart? It doesn't seem very dangerous, if you ask me.

Anyway, the man was finally convinced that I really was who I said I was, and I assured him that I would ring my parents and ask them to come to the church. As usual, my mother didn't answer her phone, but my father answered his and promised to come round immediately. Just before he arrived, my mother appeared, on her way back from a prayer meeting. Thankfully, she was wearing her dog collar, so clearly she didn't need to identify herself. The man, however, refused to tell my mother his name (hypocrite...) and, when my father turned up without a dog collar, the man accused him of not wearing his 'uniform'. My father now fondly refers to himself as 'the undercover vicar'. Take from that what you will.

So, my friends, always remember to carry ID. Either that, or never, *ever* own up to being your parents' child. To be honest, the latter will probably serve you better.

Your love life will be a continual source of parish speculation

A teenager's love life: more ups and downs than a rollercoaster, more heartbreaks than a chick flick. That's what all the adults think, anyway. A lot of the time, it's not really the case, but, as many fellow ministry children will know, that has never stopped people from asking probing questions about the ins and outs of a teenager's deep and feeling heart. Even when you insist that there is nothing to tell because you've been focused on your schoolwork, or your degree, or sport—or because you go to a single-sex school and everyone else in the church is significantly older than you—still they will query every possible interaction you might have with the opposite sex.

There are many examples I could give, from the woman who asked me and one of my male friends if we'd managed to 'get it on' yet, to another parishioner who would greet every youngish male entering the church with the question, 'Are you another one of Nell's men?' I'm sure, if I were to do some wider research, I would gather hundreds and hundreds of hilarious and cringeworthy stories about parishioners questioning, meddling with and becoming unnecessarily invested in the love lives of their clergy's offspring. But for now, I will leave you with a favourite of mine: a conversation that my mother had with a parishioner when I was 19 and made the mistake of speaking to a couple of male friends after church.

Parishioner So, is Nell dating anyone?

Mum No, she isn't.

Parishioner Are you sure about that? Isn't she dating that guy she's standing next to?

Mum No, they're just friends.

Parishioner Oh, but she's standing very close to him, closer than she is to that other man on the other side of her. They must be dating.

Mum No, they're definitely not dating.

Parishioner Well, she definitely likes him. Look how close they're standing.

Mum That's just the angle you're looking at them from. They're definitely not dating, and I'm pretty sure she doesn't like him like that. As I said, they're just friends.

Parishioner Well, he definitely likes her. He's standing very close to her; can't you see it?

Mum No, that's just the angle, really. They're not dating.

Parishioner *(Unconvinced sigh.)*

Wherever you go as a clergy child, you cannot escape the speculation. You must resign yourself to the fact that until you are safely married off, you will almost certainly be match-made with every eligible (and non-eligible) man or woman in the congregation, and continually quizzed on your non-existent 'man/lady friend'. All the more reason to keep any potential (or actual) relationships a complete secret, I'd say!

Sometimes it's just awful, but God is still good

There are some days that I like to call 'Bad Clergy Child Days'. We all know them—when you decide that you can't take it any more and you just want out. When it feels as if everything is awful and nothing is going right and there is no way to make it any better. But let me remind you that even in those moments, God is still good. Here's an example of just that.

After we'd had the church over for a barbecue one Sunday lunchtime, I discovered that my purse had been taken from my closed bag, while it was sitting in my hallway. All my bank cards, my driving licence, my National Insurance card, my 16–25 Railcard, my Nectar card, my Oyster card, everything—plus the money I had made babysitting on Friday night—taken. Gone. Just like that. That someone would come into our house, accept our hospitality, our food, our love and our time, and then, on their way out, go deliberately riffling through a handbag and take out the purse, was beyond me.

I was so angry and hurt and upset. I sat on the kitchen floor and cried and cried—and yelled. A lot. Mainly at my parents. One of my outbursts involved the words 'If this is ministry, then screw ministry! I don't want it any more. I don't care. I hate it all!' And yes, I felt like that. Sometimes it feels as if my whole life is the first part of 'Clergy child's lament' (pp. 10–12). Sometimes I do wish it all away and wish that God had put me in a 'normal' family with a 'normal' home and parents with 'normal' jobs.

But God has not called me to 'normality'. And you know what? I think that might be OK. Sometimes, in a church, it's easiest to see the difficult stuff—the broken people, the broken lives, the dishonesty, the mess. And you forget to see the beautiful things—the lives changed, the wounds healed, the broken hearts bound up, the generosity and the love for each other. When some people in the church heard that my purse had been stolen, two of them offered to pay for it to be replaced. Others gave me money to make up for the cash that was stolen. Because they care. Because they love me. Because they are lovely and generous. Because God is good, and *he* cares—for me, for my family, for the church. He even cares for the person who stole my purse. And that's why I have no choice but to forgive. Although it hurts; although it makes me angry and makes me upset and makes me feel violated and makes me want never to let anyone into my home ever again, we forgive people because God first forgave us. We love people because God first loved us, even in the depth of our failings, our denial, our lies and our mess. God first loved us, we are forgiven and therefore we are called to forgive.

So yes, sometimes it's awful. Sometimes you just want to curl up in a ball and cry and yell and scream. You hate ministry and everything to do with church and God and Christianity. But that's not the end. It's never the end. The end is God, and God is good, no matter what.

Forgive; it changes lives

Forgiveness is a word that is bandied around a lot, especially in church. But there's a reason it's mentioned so often: it's actually really important. And it's something which is particularly important to learn as a clergy child, because you're going to be hurt. You're going to be hurt by parishioners, by the church as a whole and by your parents. I wish I could put it less bluntly than that, but I can't. That's just how it is. Part of being a clergy child is getting hurt, and getting hurt by Christians.

This tip has two main points. Its overarching message is, as the title says, 'Forgive; it changes lives'. But I want to tell you that this is bigger and more significant than it may initially appear. Forgiveness, you see, doesn't just change the lives of those whom you forgive; it also changes your life. So here are two stories—one about how learning to forgive changed my life, and one about how my forgiveness of someone else changed their life.

I'll be honest with you. I used to sit through talks about loving your enemies and forgiving people, getting more and more cross with the person speaking, convinced that they didn't know what they were talking about, didn't know how angry and hurt I felt. I was adamant that I must at least receive an apology before I began to forgive.

But forgiveness doesn't work like that. As a teenager, I was confronted with this reality while sitting outside church one day, faced with a choice: forgive, lash out or ignore. The actions of the man in question had resulted in my parents losing their jobs, and us as a family losing our home and leaving the city we had lived in for nine years.

I'd come back to visit my old church friends that weekend—the first time I'd been back since we'd been forced to move. As this man, the one whose actions had turned my world upside down, walked past me, I wrestled with God. Almost every part of me wanted to go up and punch him in the face. A quiet voice told me to offer my hand in forgiveness.

I wish I could tell you that I forgave him that day. I wish I could tell you I walked up to him with my hand outstretched, looked him in the eye and said those three powerful words, 'I forgive you.' But I didn't. I let him walk past me without so much as a glance in my direction. I justified my inaction by telling myself that I would forgive him when it hurt less. It was still too raw, I thought. The anger still weighed too heavily on my soul.

The thing is, though, that the anger nearly destroyed me completely. That unforgiveness, which I had been so quick to justify, remained buried inside me. Years later, I battled with depression, anxiety and eating problems. I hated myself. I lost a stone in just over a month. I slept for 15 hours a day. On more than one occasion the darkness was so heavy that it came close to overwhelming me completely. I had reached the end of myself.

I flung myself at the foot of the cross, begging for Jesus to take those feelings from me. The response I got was one word: 'Forgive'. I knew what it meant, but my emotions raged against it. It still hurt too much. I was still too angry, too upset, too bitter. But no longer could I bear the all-encompassing weight. It had become too much.

So, with a deep breath and a lot of tears, I got down on my knees and began to pray. I asked for forgiveness for myself, and began to ask God to teach me, in the knowledge of his forgiveness of me, how to forgive others. Forgiving this particular person didn't just mean a one-off prayer of 'God bless X', which was hard enough to say. Praying for him meant asking God to give me the strength and courage to forgive him. It meant asking God to give him everything I wanted for myself. With the patient encouragement of a dear friend, I prayed that my ceiling would be this man's floor. I prayed for his children. I prayed blessings over his marriage, his family, his home. I cried and I prayed and I began to learn to forgive, and the weight was lifted. As I prayed, God's grace took the burden of the emotion and the darkness from around my shoulders and hung it on the cross.

Forgiveness is not something that can be given out of human strength. It cannot be done from sheer willpower. It must be done in the knowledge and security of God's love for you, his forgiveness of all your sins, and his love and forgiveness of the one who has wronged you as well.

A few years later, I was still learning to forgive. It was a daily choice not to pick up the burden of bitterness, anger and resentment that I had carried for so long. Then came an experience which reminded me that forgiveness just doesn't change the life of the one who forgives; it also has the power to radically alter the life of the one forgiven.

My purse was stolen. Perhaps you've read about it in the previous tip, 'Sometimes it's just awful, but God is still good'. We soon thought we knew who we had to talk to about the incident. It was someone who had a history of theft; they weren't a Christian yet, and they had been kicked out of other churches for being 'unmanageable'. I was angry. There's no point in denying it. I was mad. My money had been taken, and it felt as if the hospitality we'd offered had been violated and abused.

A few days afterwards, my mum sat me down and told me that someone had admitted to taking my purse. It was the person we'd thought it was, but that didn't make it any easier. The person wanted to talk to me about it that Sunday after church. I was still really cross and hurt. It was unfair, and a large part of me longed for justice: they should have to pay back the money, everyone should know what they'd done, and they should have to make a public apology. The irrationality of my anger knew no bounds.

But I also knew that I had to forgive. Having let opportunities to forgive pass me by previously, and in the knowledge of the power of forgiveness for my own life, I knew I had to ask God for the strength to forgive this person too.

Sunday rolled around, and after the service I sat down with this person and with my mum. With some gentle encouragement, they looked me in the eye, told me what they'd done and asked for my forgiveness. They said they'd taken the money and thrown the purse itself away, so they couldn't get it back, but they would like to try to repay the money.

I knew this person couldn't afford to repay it. I looked down and swallowed. I knew what the Bible said: 'Freely you have received; freely give' (Matthew 10:8). 'Forgive each other, just as in Christ God forgave you' (Ephesians 4:32). I knew I had to do it, but it was hard. I uttered a silent prayer for strength, raised my eyes to theirs, and said the words that I had failed to say to others before: 'I forgive you.' More than that, I heard myself saying that there was no need to pay back the money; it didn't matter. All that mattered was that I forgave.

The person was baffled—completely perplexed. 'But why?' they asked. 'Why would you forgive me? How can you do that? Why don't you want the money back? Why are you being so kind?' I told them the truth: it wasn't me; it was God. I couldn't forgive them on my own or love them on my own. I could only do it because God had forgiven me and loved me first—because he forgave them and loved them, and was helping me to do the same, right there and then. With eyes full of tears, the person stood up and hugged me. We parted ways for that evening, and a peace reigned in my soul that I had never expected.

The next week, that person gave their life to Jesus. So amazed were they by my offer of forgiveness and my declaration that it was because of what God had done for me, and because of God's love for them, they decided they wanted to be in. And as if that wasn't enough, they came into church every week for the next month or so with handfuls of stuff they had stolen and returned those things to the church, or to individuals, with apologies and requests for forgiveness. They haven't stolen a single thing since that day, over three years ago.

Forgiveness doesn't just change you; it changes other people as well. It changes lives and alters paths and shows people that Jesus is the most powerful way possible. Forgiveness is countercultural, against everything our world tells us about rights and justice. But it will set you free in ways you couldn't have dreamed, and it will empower others in extraordinary ways as well. So please, if there is one thing that you take away from this book, let it be this: forgive. It will change your life and the lives of others around you in incredible, unexpected, immeasurable, powerful ways.

Letters

Dear Friend,

Welcome to section two: 'Letters'. As you may well have guessed, this section is written as correspondence to you, addressing particular situations that you may encounter as life goes on. It aims to offer some practical advice, as well as assuring you that you are not alone. I hope it will encourage you to see where God has been at work in situations and circumstances throughout your life, to develop an understanding of his faithfulness and his grace, and to learn something of his character.

This section is a lot more emotionally exposing than 'Tips' and addresses some tricky topics, but I promise that you will never be left in a place of despair; with God there is always hope. I will try my utmost to reflect that truth in everything I write to you, and I pray that as you journey through life, through many situations not addressed in this section, you will learn that you cannot be overwhelmed because you are hidden with Christ in God.

I don't expect you to read this section in one sitting; it's an awful lot to process all at once. Plus, I assume that some of the letters will be relevant for you and others really won't. That being said, however, even if you don't relate to them, you will probably one day encounter someone to whom they do relate, so read them nonetheless. Pray about them, think them through and be willing to learn something of God and of life, and of how they intersect in the most beautiful of ways.

If you ever want to write back to me, I'd love to hear from you! You can contact me through my blog, the details of which can be found on the back cover of this book.

I'm praying for you.

Love, Nell x

A letter for the new clergy child

Dear Friend,

It's a strange time in your life right now. A season of change—a new house, a new church, maybe a new school and a whole host of new emotions. I know that there are so many different thoughts and feelings running through your head and your heart as you read this. I know that nothing feels quite right, and it all seems a bit unsettled. I know you're probably an overwhelming mix of proud and excited and just a little bit scared. I know that you might be feeling quite angry and resentful because you never really wanted this change, and it might sometimes feel as if God has forgotten you in his calling of your parents.

I know that it's strange to have your dad or your mum at the front, leading the service, preaching and giving out Communion, instead of sitting with you in the pews, like he or she always did before. I know that your dad's new dog collar is a strange addition to his outfit, and you're still not quite used to it. I know that you still secretly want to laugh at the fact that your dad is wearing a dog collar, because it does, quite frankly, sound ridiculous.

I know that you're unsure what to expect from the people in your new church—the ones who talk to you as if they already know everything about you, who smile at you and hug you and are overwhelmingly lovely to you all of the time. I know that it feels strange to be the centre of attention, to be asked questions and not know which answer to give—the honest one or the one they expect to hear. I know that you're bursting with pride to see how well loved your dad or mum is by everyone around, but I also know that this comes with a strange twinge of jealousy, an anxiety that maybe you're going to lose him or her to them.

I know that, actually, your new church might not be quite as friendly as that. There might not be many other people your own age, and you're worried about making friends and starting over in a brand-new place. I know that you notice the moments of tension and stress at home more than anyone thinks you do. I know you overhear conversations that you know you shouldn't. I know that you're far too good at keeping secrets already, and you've not been around all that long yet. I know that you have so many mixed emotions about moving house and church and maybe even school, and that sometimes it feels as if God stole your parents, your home and all that you had previously known and loved.

I know that your new house feels unnaturally large, and it seems odd to have so many people in and out of it all the time. I know it's weird to have the doorbell or the phone always ringing, to never be sure of what to say to the strangers who arrive before the previous meeting has finished. I know that you're unsure how many of your childhood antics will be exposed in this week's sermon illustration. I know that, sometimes, you feel as if you don't really know anything at all any more.

I'm not going to promise you that life as a clergy child will be easy. There will be days when you want to curl up in a ball and cry, wishing that everyone would go away and leave your family in peace. There will be moments when you want to yell at people, to use your words as weapons rather than as gifts, and times when you will bite your tongue moments before you say something deeply hurtful. There will be people who ask questions they have no right to know the answers to, and you will want to ask equally obtuse questions in return, just to show them how it feels. There will be Sundays when you're on three different rotas and you'll feel as if there isn't enough of you to go round. There will be vicarage lunches where you sit quietly, resenting the small talk you must make with those around you. There will be seasons when you question whether God really knew what he was doing when he called your parents and your family to ordination, to this church, to this crazy and unpredictable life.

But what I can promise you is that this life will inspire you. It will grow you and change you and teach you things you never thought it possible to learn. It will show you first-hand the wonders of how God changes lives. It will give you stories to tell at dinner parties for years to come. It will never cease to amaze you. You are going to see lives changed beyond recognition. You are going to discover just how much love you have to give. You are going to learn how to forgive and how to hope and how to have grace even when it feels as if there isn't an ounce of graciousness left within you.

You will meet people who drive you crazy and people who show you love in ways you never expected. People who make you feel things you never thought it was possible to feel. People who turn you inside out and upside down and who you will care for so deeply that you can't begin to express it. You will see humility and generosity daily, and you will be astounded by the magnitude of people's ability to deal with all that life throws at them. You will befriend those to whom you would never usually think of speaking. You will share the most precious moments of your life—Christmas, Easter, birthdays—with people who will change your perspective on the world for ever. You will learn things that stay with you for the rest of your life. You will cry through the funerals of people with whom you have shared more Christmases than with your own grandparents. You will laugh at the baptisms of children whose parents' love you saw blossom over years, and whose wedding you remember as if it were yesterday. You will garner life skills such as cooking lunch for 15 at two hours' notice, keeping a straight face when accepting the most random of gifts, and the ability to maintain a ten-minute conversation about the liturgical significance of ice cream.

Most importantly, though, you will see something of God every single day. You will find him in the people you meet, the conversations you have, the cakes you bake, the cards you receive, the questions you answer, the small talk you make and the silences you sit through. You will find him in the quietest, most unlikely of places. You will find him even in the questions, the doubt, the anger and the turmoil—in the uncertainty and distrust, the pain and the tears. When you reach the end of yourself—which you will, because a vicarage is not an easy place to be—you will find him there, with open arms and kind eyes, gentle words and a peaceful presence.

My friend, I am not promising you an easy ride or all the answers to the questions you're too scared to ask. I am not promising that the unnameable emotions that currently threaten to overwhelm you will be gone come morning. But what I can promise you is that God will always be enough. When you are scared, remind yourself of his perfect love for you. When you are doubting, listen for that quiet voice of truth whispering through the noise of the questions. When you are lonely, let him enfold you in his arms. When you don't know what to do, remember that he has great plans for you. When you feel forgotten or overlooked, discover again the truth of his acceptance of you.

Do not be afraid, my friend. You are embarking on the adventure of a lifetime, and you have the king of the universe as your travel companion. It's going to be OK.

I'm praying for you.

Love, Nell x

A letter for clergy parents

Dear Friend,

I know this is a book for clergy children and those who are growing up in Christian homes, but I guess that some of you reading it might be more 'young at heart' than actually young. And I realise that the title, *Musings of a Clergy Child*, has probably attracted the readership of a fair few clergy parents. After all, which vicar parent doesn't want some insights into what it's like to grow up in a vicarage? So if that is you, real-life adult and maybe even real-life Reverend adult, welcome. It's so lovely to have you here. This letter is for you.

Let me begin by stating what I hope you already know: I am not a parent and I am not a professional. I have never raised children and I've never had any training on how one might go about doing that. These tips are merely what I have learnt from my own upbringing, from talking to other clergy kids and from discussing things with my parents. They are not hard-and-fast rules; they are not black-and-white decrees. They are merely suggestions, advice, thoughts from the journey of growing up in ministry.

The first and most important thing to remember is, I hope, obvious: your ministry and your parenting are two different things. They are two separate entities that have come together. Maybe sometimes your church feels like your other, bigger, louder, needier child, but it's really not. Your ministry and your parenting are two separate callings. It's up to you to decide whether one has priority over the other. Some say family comes first; others hold both equally—but you must never blend the two areas into one, because to do that is to undermine both.

Off the back of that, I have five top tips for you as you try to juggle being both a parent and a vicar in everyday life. They will not solve all your problems, nor will they all apply to you, but I hope and pray that even one or two of them will help you think through what it means to be the parent of someone growing up in the goldfish bowl of ministry life.

Involve your children in decisions

I cannot begin to emphasise how important this is. For as long as I can remember, my parents have always talked to me and my brother about everything that's been going on, no matter how serious or painful it has been. No decision is too big for a child not to be given an input, no matter how young, immature or shy they are. If you don't involve your children in your decisions, you are treading a very dangerous path. Surely, if you're involved in ministry, you want your children to be supporting you? If you don't let them have a say in decisions, they won't actively support those decisions, because they won't feel as if they have the autonomy to do so. Respect your children as individuals, be honest with them and be willing to reconsider your views in the light of their thoughts on the matter. This comes from a place of relationship: no one has a veto and no one has a trump card. It's a team decision!

Let's take my family's move to London as an example. Before my parents even started to look at parish profiles, they sat me and my brother down and said that they wanted to talk seriously together about the possibility of moving. My mum didn't have a job, my dad was the sole breadwinner and they felt quite strongly that it was time to look outside Bristol. Now, my brother and I were very happy in Bristol: it felt like home in ways that few other places ever have done. We had a lovely church, good friends and brilliant schools. But our parents weren't entirely happy, so we sat down as a family and we talked and prayed about it. We thrashed it out together. We really talked, and our parents really listened. They took into account what we said: we don't want you to look at places that are too far away from Bristol; we don't want to be in the middle of nowhere; and I want a school place before we move. These feelings were taken into consideration by our parents, and this meant that when we made a decision to move, we made it as a family. It wasn't a case of me and my brother submitting to our parents; it was a case of making a family decision, a team decision. This means that wherever we go and whatever we do, we know we're a team and we're in it together, as a family. In my mind, that's something very special.

Your children will see and hear everything—so talk about it with them

A lot of children are far more intuitive than their parents give them credit for. They pick up on emotions and tensions within the home and at church. In addition, children will overhear conversations: that's just how life works. But it's extra significant in a vicarage, because clergy children overhear a wide variety of discussions—from people struggling with depression and suicidal thoughts to people talking about their sex lives during marriage preparation. Even for an adult or teenager, this is a lot to take in, but for a child, it needs to be explained. It needs to be talked through and worked through and properly addressed. It's so important that a clergy child feels free to ask questions—whether about mental illness, sex, God, faith, doubt, love, joy, hope, exorcisms, cave men or dinosaurs (all of which have been dinner-time conversation topics in my house). And if your child overhears something confidential, tell them that it should go no further. A child understands the idea of keeping a secret. Don't shut your children out of your ministry: they'll come to resent it if you do. Embrace them and their awkward questions wholeheartedly, and I doubt you'll ever regret it.

For example, I remember when my mum was a chaplain at an Oxford college. One morning, aged about seven, I woke up to find that she wasn't at home. I asked Dad where she had gone and he quietly explained to me that during the night, a student had tried to commit suicide, so she'd had to go and visit them in hospital. This was my first contact with death and suicide, so naturally I had a lot of questions, just as any child would. It would have been so easy for my dad (and my mum, for she got inundated with questions when she came home) to brush off my questions by telling me it was 'grown-up stuff' and that I would 'understand when I was older'. But no, they answered all my questions as best they could, while still respecting my age and emotional immaturity. Then we sat down and prayed for the student and the student's family.

I suppose, in some cases, the default position for any parent is to protect their children from anything that could hurt them or mess up their view of the world. But growing up in a vicarage means that children will hear of hurtful things; they will see just how horrid the world can be, and they'll be curious about it. So they'll ask questions. If they're shunned and told not to ask difficult questions, or to stop being nosy, goodness knows what will happen—but it certainly won't be good. But if their questions are answered with love and care, and they remain secure in the knowledge that life can be dreadful but it's OK to talk about it, they can learn more life lessons in a day than they would in a year of being told they're 'too young to understand'. Trust me: by addressing your children's questions properly instead of wrapping them in cotton wool and skirting around the issues, you're doing them a favour.

Share your struggles, but also share your victories

Life as a vicar is tough. Everyone knows that, and no one more so than a clergy child. As aforementioned, children are perceptive: they pick up on problems, even if you think you are doing a good job of hiding them. So be open with your struggles. Ask your children to pray for you if you've got a particularly difficult meeting coming up: they'll be excited to know that you value their prayers and you want them to help you.

But make sure that you're not just sharing your struggles. Share your victories too. Did the meeting go well? Tell them. Someone became a Christian? Let them know. Your sermon has been written before Sunday morning? Give them a high-five. The person they overheard you talking about, who was struggling with addiction, has been clean for a whole month? Let them join in the celebration.

Let your children be selfish about their time with you

As a vicar, you'll be a busy person. As a parent, you'll be equally busy. Juggling the two roles can be hard. But remember that your church is made up of lots of people who can do things to help the needy as well; only you can be your child's mother or father. So let them be selfish with you sometimes. Not all the time, because that's silly, but sometimes. Set aside some time each day to spend with your children—walking the dog in the morning together or sitting down before bed to watch a TV programme. Let them answer the phone on your day off and ban anyone else from talking to you because it's your time with them. My mum's dad, who was also a vicar, used to have one day a year when he took each of his four children away for the day, for a special treat. There's nothing more important than your children. If someone arrives at your door wanting something on your day off, when you're spending time with your family, let someone else help them. Your child only has you, whereas the upset parishioner has the curate or the pastoral assistant or the Licensed Lay Minister. Obviously this selfishness should not be excessive, but boundaries are excellent, both for clergy children and for clergy parents themselves.

Make sure your child feels safe

Vicarages can be really scary places, especially if you're home alone in one. They're massive and dark, and lots of people know where you live. So make sure that your child feels safe. No matter how irrational their fear, acknowledge it and find a way to placate it. A male parishioner is making your teenage daughter uncomfortable? Make sure she's never placed in a situation on her own with him. Your son dislikes other people using his mugs? Put them on a separate shelf. The doorbell rings when they're home alone? Tell them they don't have to answer it. Persistent ringing of the doorbell? Make sure they know where the panic button is.

Think of it this way: if your child was scared of the dark, which is admittedly a somewhat irrational fear, you wouldn't leave them to sleep alone in a dark room without a nightlight or the door open. The same applies to vicarages—they can be scary. Don't leave teenagers alone there without a method of coping and an emergency contingency plan. It's as simple as that.

I suppose this letter boils down to communication. Communicate with your children. Answer their questions. Treat their worries seriously. Protect them and honour them with the truth. Make sure they know what's going on. Often, as a child of people in ministry, a lot of things feel as if they are out of control, so make sure they don't feel that way about the important things. Talk to them. Take a break from your sermon-writing to give them a cuddle when they ask for one. And, most importantly of all, pray with them. Lead them to God, as he's the one you're working for, he's the one who has called you, and ultimately he's the only one who will never let your children down. If they don't understand the nature of the God whom you serve, the God you long for them to know and trust as their own Lord and saviour, they'll never truly understand the nature of your whole life.

This isn't an easy journey. I know that, and I'm not even a parent in ministry. I don't have the answer, but I hope and pray that a little of what is written here has helped and blessed you in some way. Keep going; you're doing a great job.

I'm praying for you and for your family.

Love, Nell x

A letter for when the church has hurt you

Dear Friend,

I do not know what has been said or done to you which means that you find yourself needing to read this letter. I'm not going to tell you I understand, because I don't and I probably never will. But let me say, first of all, that I am sorry. I am sorry for words said, or not said; for things done, or not done; for actions, consequences, blame, anger, unforgiveness, manipulation, blackmail or abuse. I am so, so sorry. I do not have a simple answer to your pain. I do not have a magic word or a quick formula to make it better, to make the pain go away. All I have to offer you is Jesus. He is not who the church has often presented him to be. He is love, forgiveness, grace, mercy, tenderness and kindness. He is the living embodiment of God himself—the God who created you, who knows you, who loves you. The God who sees all that goes on in his church and weeps with you over it; he weeps for you in your pain. He draws close to you and walks by your side, carrying you when all strength has gone. He is there. He sees. He knows.

This letter to you contains a story, because the only way I know to relate to you in this is to tell you something of my journey, a snippet of the hurt that a part of the church caused me and my family. Your pain is personal. The way the church has hurt you is personal and unique to you. I cannot ever fully understand the depth and breadth of the hurt you have experienced, because I am not you. I do not know who caused you pain—whether it was one Christian or a whole church community. I do not know if it was a one-off experience or if it is an ongoing battle. I do not know the ins and outs of your pain, and I will not pretend that I do. I will only tell you a part of my story, a part of my struggle. I will only aim to show you that you are not alone.

There isn't a simple answer to your pain, but there is Jesus. Jesus remains, no matter what pain surrounds you, no matter what the actions of the church have been or those who call themselves Jesus' followers. Let me tell you a little of how I learnt that, no matter what, still he remains.

◆ ◆ ◆

I find myself standing alone in a playpark, the drizzle mixing with my tears. My stomach is churning and my head is buzzing. Questions fly from my head to my heart and back again. So rarely are the two connected, and yet today, the feelings and questions are all jumbled up in a tight knot, making me ever so aware of how little I understand myself and how little I understand God.

I never realised that pain could be recurrent until this day. The questions I thought I'd answered years ago come racing to the forefront of my mind, as burning as they ever were, the previous answers lying forgotten by the wayside.

I'm standing alone in a playpark. A seemingly harmless conversation with a church representative has sent me hurtling back six, seven, eight years, to a time when I began to doubt the rock upon which I had built my life. That rock was being chipped away, day after day, by another Christian. The rock of knowing who God was, of assuming that God's people always acted in a particular way and that the Bible was used to build people up was being eroded. Here the Bible was being used to manipulate, harm and destroy.

I didn't understand. From the age of 11 through to 14 and beyond, I didn't understand how people who claimed to follow the same God as me could have such a radically different view of his purpose and plan. God seemingly stood, distant and cold, behind a dark cloud of my resentment, anger and confusion—and I gave up on him. Refusing to believe in the same God as the person who was taking away everything I knew and loved, I turned my back and walked in the opposite direction.

But still he remained.

He was an ever-present help in trouble, the one I could not forget, no matter how hard I tried. Still he was there, shining brightly with love, peace and forgiveness behind the dark cloud with which he had been covered—man of sorrows, acquainted with grief.

I've never understood how God works. I long to know how he takes all that is bad, all that hurts and all that weighs heavily upon me, and turns it, ever so slowly, into something beautiful. I want to be able to explain how he is found in the smallest things, making the biggest impact.

He was there in the darkness of my early teenage years, in the questioning and the anger. He was there, feeling with me every blow that came to the rock upon which I was standing, holding me tightly as I struggled to stand. He was there in the move from the home I loved, in the stress-induced sickness of my mother, in the resentment and the tears and the confusion. He was there. I just couldn't always see him, because suddenly he was not as easily understood. The God of my childhood, of simple Sunday school stories, was gone. He had been replaced by a God no less incredible, but one darkened by questions and blurred by tears of red-hot fury and hurt.

But still he remained.

He was to be found in the quietest, most unlikely of places: in the house by the Irish Sea that was lent to us by former colleagues; in the Marks & Spencer food vouchers given to make life easier as my mother caught illness after illness; in the friend who cooked me dinner as I sat on his kitchen floor, quietly sobbing into my tea.

Still he remained.

He was there as I found myself, years later, standing alone in a playpark. He was there as the drizzle mixed with my tears. The questions that I never really answered danced in front of my eyes, mocking me. But this time, I looked closer. I looked closer for my God. The one who is found in the unexpected places, who seems to be hiding but is actually closer than ever before.

He is to be found in a revision companion's listening ear and in the quiet prayer uttered as you sit together on the floor of a church cloakroom, eyes moist and hearts troubled. He is to be found in the phone call from a friend who read between the lines of a text and cared enough to call. But he is to be found, most clearly of all, in the previously undiscovered passages of the book you assumed was only for those who had it sorted—in the depths of his word.

> I remember my affliction and my wandering,
>   the bitterness and the gall.
> I well remember them,
>   and my soul is downcast within me.
> Yet this I call to mind
>   and therefore I have hope:
> Because of the Lord's great love we are not consumed,
>   for his compassions never fail.
> They are new every morning;
>   great is your faithfulness.
> LAMENTATIONS 3:19–23

Standing, alone, in a play park. Still he remains.

Wherever you are, wherever you find yourself in your pain, still he remains.

I'm praying for you.

Love, Nell x

A letter for when you feel as if the church has stolen your parents

Dear Friend,

I must begin my letter to you with a small preface. This letter is for the moments when you feel as if the church has stolen your parents. It's for those moments when you are angry at God and you are angry at the church, because it's not fair and other people are getting more attention from your family than you are. This is a letter about how it can sometimes feel to be a child of parents in ministry, not only from my own experience but from the experience of fellow clergy children with whom I have spoken and journeyed. It is not a confession of my parents' neglect or failings; they have been more wonderful to me than I can say. But parents are human, just like the rest of us, and so they hurt us, just in the same way that we hurt them. When you are the child of someone in ministry, that hurt is tangled up with a whole host of other emotions, some too deep-seated and confusing to put into words.

This letter is not a confession or a lecture. It is not an answer to all your questions or a solution to all your problems. It is deeply personal, written from my heart to yours, to show you that you are not alone in these emotions, and that sometimes we just have to listen to the truth of who God says we are, rather than the lies that want to shape our hearts.

To the one reading this with tears in your eyes and a lump in your throat, with anger in your heart and rejection heavy on your back: this is for you.

You may have heard it said as many times as I did growing up: as a child of those in ministry, you will go one of two ways. Perhaps you will be 'good'. You might have a few rocky patches along the way, but you will have your own faith; you will be well-behaved and well-mannered, able to talk to old ladies and small children alike; and you will probably end up in some form of ministry yourself. Alternatively, you will rebel—go off the rails, completely and utterly. You will turn your back on God, on religion, on your parents' advice and on the lessons you've been taught. You will get to a point where you know everything so well that you can argue with any point presented to you, but the belief is non-existent and God seems very far away.

It seems strange that these polar opposites can come from the same kind of upbringing. Those on the outside often don't really understand. How can one sibling turn out so 'good' and the other so deeply rebellious? How can one of you have all the answers and the other have nothing but questions?

Deep down, though, I think you know the answer. It took me a while—days and months and years of wrestling and questioning, of battling with fear and rejection, guilt and betrayal. It took sleepless nights and many, many tears. But then I realised: it felt as if God stole my parents. It feels, sometimes, as if God has taken them away and forgotten about me in the midst of their calling.

God stole your parents. You see, ministry is a vocation, and the calling is clear to those who are ordained: that is their life's work. Often, those who are called feel an overwhelming duty to fulfil the calling. This is an amazing thing; it changes lives and blesses people and furthers the kingdom of God. That must not be forgotten. But it means that ministry can become all-encompassing. Ministry cannot, by its very nature, be a 9–5 desk job, no matter how much the person in ministry might want it to be. No matter how hard they try, ministry is not something that can be 'left at the office'. Their home is the place from which the ministry takes place, and their life is filled with people, PCC meetings and pastoral emergencies.

And you, as a child of those in ministry, don't really have a choice in the matter. You have been sucked into ministry whether you like it or not. Some thrive, but others resent. You, after all, did not choose to be in ministry, but it often feels as if that's what you have to be. On top of that, it can frequently feel as if you are in competition. You end up having some kind of strange sibling rivalry with your parents' church. You feel as if you have to compete with more than 100 other people who are far needier, far louder and far more demanding than you could ever be. And, because vicars are human too, they often end up listening to the one who shouts loudest and forget to hear the quiet voice of their child, just as needy but drowned out by the din of parishioners' pastoral problems. Then, because you are also human, you remember only the times when your parents put other people first, and you never see the incredible sacrifices made by your parents for you over the hundreds of others.

So you turn away. You stop asking for your parents' attention because you think you will never be able to compete with everyone else who is demanding it. And, as you stop asking, you start believing the lies that are whispered to you in the darkness of the night and the silence of the doubt. The lie that your parents care more about their ministry than they do about their children. The lies that God cares more about the church than he does about individuals, and that God's call on your parents' life was a calling away from you. The lie that God stole your parents.

Stop for a minute, and listen. There is something within you that fights back. No, it says, God is not like that. There is more to him than his call on your parents' life. He cares about individuals. He made individuals. He loves the church, but he also loves individuals. He is the father to the fatherless. He calls every person to himself and provides for all that he has made. He plans for each individual, regardless of who their parents are or what they have done. He leads with cords of human kindness, with ties of love. He is not only the creator but the sustainer of all.

And so the battle rages. The truth and the lies go round and round, competing for attention, for belief, for investment—competing for the very core of your being, for your devotion. There are days when the truth wins, and there are days when the lies dominate. For some, it is far more of one than the other. When the lies dominate, acceptance must be found elsewhere, and God is a monster. God is shrouded in lies and you want nothing to do with him. So you run and hide, wherever you can.

But when the truth wins, there is freedom. There is liberation from the lies. There is the ability to see your parents as human beings and love them anyway. You are able to acknowledge that your parents have not always got it right, but they've tried their very best. And God fills in where your parents have failed. God's grace goes further. It covers not only your parents' mistakes but also the lies you have believed.

Then comes the choice between the truth and the lies, the choice between acceptance and rejection. Choose the truth and reject the lies, or believe the lies and forget the truth.

To those on the outside, it seems so simple. Make the choice, go with the truth and live in the knowledge of it. But I know that, for you, this is not just a one-off, split-second decision. It is a daily battle, an hourly choice. It is a war that rages within you, day in, day out, a tug of war in which you are the rope. There are days when the lies shout so loudly that you cannot hear even the faintest whisper of the truth. Then there are days when the truth seems so glaringly obvious that you cannot imagine a world in which the lies could win. But most days, it is a battle—a fierce war between the truth and the lies. Round and round, in and out, over and under—inescapable and unfathomable.

But the beauty of the truth, you see, is that it prevails. It remains the truth, whether or not you choose to accept it. And there is always a way back to the truth, no matter how long you have believed the lies.

There is grace, there is redemption and there is freedom. You need only look to the truth, and the truth will set you free.

So, my friend, let me take a moment to write the truth to you. Hold it close to your heart and remember it when the lies are so loud that you can no longer hear anything else.

God has not stolen your parents. The lies have. God has called your parents, yes, but not away from you. You, as their child, are a key part of their calling. God is faithful and true; the lies are not. God loves you and protects you and wants the best for you, and so do your parents. They are called not only to be in ministry but also to be your parents. Do not believe the lies that tell you otherwise. When your parents fail, and they inevitably will because they are human, God will not. He will never fail. So lay your burdens, your pain, your anger and your lies at the foot of the cross, and look to the truth of God's love for you as an individual. You are a beloved child of his, redeemed, forgiven and looked after, no matter what.

I'm praying for you.

Love, Nell x

A letter for when someone leaves

Dear Friend,

It hurts. Don't lie to yourself. Don't tell yourself it will all be OK if you just ignore the fact that things are changing. Don't ignore the knots in your stomach, the sinking of your heart every time you think of what is drawing ever closer. Do not stifle the salty tears that threaten to spill over when you remember what is to come. Do not gloss over the misplaced anger at those who are taking your friend away; do not skirt over the knowledge that, really, you're angry not at the people but at the change itself. Do not do yourself such a disservice as to believe the lie that friendships are static, that they will always remain the same. Do not think that if you change, you will lose everything.

No matter how much it hurts, take the time to listen as your friend stands in front of you and asks you, ever so gently, to set them free. Listen to the voice of the friend who intertwined their life with yours; who became as family; who laughed with you, cried with you and has taught you more about friendship, love and life, than you ever thought possible. Listen as they ask you quietly, gently and lovingly one of the hardest questions you will ever have to answer: 'Will you let me go?'

I know there is a battle raging. I know that you do not wish to let go, that this friendship feels safe where it is. Where it is, you understand it; you can make sense of it. This is how it was given to you, how it came. You have invested in it, cared for it and watched quietly as it grew into something beautiful. And you have loved it. Oh, how you have loved it.

But now, now you are being asked to learn to love in a different way—a way that doesn't depend on hourly, daily or weekly interaction, but endures through months and months spent apart. This love needs to stretch miles upon miles, to embrace other people, to encompass those your friend has chosen to love. It is no less important, no less significant, but it hurts.

Oh, how it hurts to let someone go. Oh, the fear that paralyses as you clutch and grasp at what you so desperately want to keep a hold on. And yet, as you hold on, you know that the place where your friend needs to be is away from you. You know that away from you they will flourish; away from you is the place where, for now, they are called to be. You relinquish the control; you relinquish all that once was, all that you love, and you commit to learning to love in a new way—a way that empowers them to reach their full potential. You let your friend go to a place where they will learn to be the person they have been created to be, the person they are called to be. You love in a way that keeps hold of the memories, those sweet, golden, happy memories, but lets go of the person with whom you made these memories and releases them into something new.

A friend like this will not go until you let them, you see. They care so deeply for you that they cannot bear to leave if you will not let them go, if you will not embrace the change that needs to happen. They will leave a part of themselves with you unless you give them permission to take it all and begin to grow fully as they learn. You must take a deep breath, relinquish control and trust. Trust that as you let them go, they will one day return. They will be the same person, but a better version of themselves. They will be fulfilled and free. Trust that as you let them go, you are not letting them fall. You are not abandoning, you are not forsaking, but you are loving, empowering, releasing and trusting.

As you let them go, you know that they are safe in the everlasting arms of God. The God who has asked you to release them is the same God who created them, who knows them intimately and loves them more than you ever could. And with that knowledge, you can trust.

It hurts to let people go. It hurts to set people free from the grasp of what you thought would remain for ever. It is hard to learn a new way to love those you care most about. And yet, as you do, you will not only see them find their true potential, their freedom, but you too will find yours.

There is, you see, a time for everything: 'a time to seek, and a time to lose; a time to keep, and a time to cast away' (Ecclesiastes 3:6, ESV). So we must let go of those we love, for they are worth more than the love we alone can give them. They have far more potential than that which can be reached from our control over them; they are more than the person we desire them to be. They have more lives to impact than ours alone. We must practise the art of letting go, in the knowledge that the Lord gives and the Lord takes away, but ultimately we can only love them because he loved them first.

I'm praying for you.

Love, Nell x

A letter for when you feel inadequate

Dear Friend,

'Enough' is a funny word, isn't it? Not only is it spelt as if it should be pronounced 'en-oo-guh', but it signifies a place that I'm not sure we can ever really reach. 'Enough' is a word for cooking or craft or writing essays—enough flour, enough thread, enough words—and yet it is something we so often seek for ourselves. We long to be 'enough'.

I don't know what 'enough' looks like, but I've spent most of my life chasing it. Running in circles, chasing my tail, I've been seeking and searching and aspiring for 'enough'. Good enough, thin enough, clever enough, pretty enough, fast enough, thoughtful enough, loud enough, quiet enough, friendly enough... the list goes on. I have searched high and low for what 'enough' looks like, and I have always failed to reach it.

The search for 'enough' has infiltrated every part of my life: school, university, friendships, family and hobbies. The temptation of it never leaves my mind. It follows me everywhere, clinging to my back and drowning out any thought of enjoyment. Even as I sit here in my kitchen, writing these words with a cup of tea in my hand and my dog by my side, I wonder if what I'm putting down on paper will be 'enough'.

This search has especially affected my faith. I have never felt as if I am 'enough' for God. I have brought myself, time and time again, in prayer, to the throne of the Father, and stopped myself mid-sentence. I have made my excuses and backed quietly away. I have assured him, as I remove myself from his presence, that I will return when I am good enough, thin enough, clever enough, pretty enough, fast enough, thoughtful enough, loud enough, quiet enough, friendly enough, holy enough… When I no longer feel inadequate, I say, I will return and begin again my relationship with him.

I thought that being 'enough' was the same as being loved, you see. I believed the lie that you could only be truly, deeply, fully and unconditionally loved if you were 'enough'—if you had fulfilled the criteria, ticked off the checklist, completed all the paperwork and presented official evidence to prove your point. I thought 'loved' and 'enough' were the same thing, in different words.

But they are not.

It seems strange to write this as if it is a truth that I believe every moment of every day. It is not. I am not sorted, I do not have the answers and my default belief, so often, is still 'I am not enough'. It has become the mantra of my tiredness, the go-to phrase of my insecurity. I know I am not alone in this. I know that some of you reading these words will know the heavy feeling of inadequacy, the weight of self-doubt. It will chase you through your days, constantly reminding you that you will never find 'enough', never reach perfection. You are setting yourself goals that are humanly impossible to meet, making yourself think that you will not be truly, deeply, fully and unconditionally loved until you are 'enough'.

But this is not true.

The truth is that you are already loved—fully known, and fully loved. In all your inadequacies, insecurities, failures and confusion, the Father calls you loved.

He calls you loved.

This love is not about being 'enough'; it is not about reaching particular goals or achievements. 'Loved' is not synonymous with 'enough'. You were loved before you could even spell 'enough', before you could pronounce it correctly, before you even knew how to speak. Before anyone else knew you existed, you were completely loved by the Father. God's love for you has unfathomable heights and unreachable depths that 'enough' cannot even begin to contend with. This love is not conditional on 'enough'.

And yet, even in the knowledge that I am loved, my quest for 'enough' continues. I long to prove myself worthy of this love which has been freely given. I search high and low for accolades and achievements, for I am still living in the lie that I could perhaps, one day, achieve 'enough' by myself.

But then, in his love, God whispers the truth in my ear, quietly and gently. He speaks honestly to my troubled mind: '"Enough" is impossible for you. On your own, you are helpless in the face of "enough".'

I am shattered. Who am I if I am not seeking to be 'enough'? What am I aiming for if 'enough' is no longer possible? I cannot reach it on my own, and therefore I do not know what to do.

But there is more. There is more after the bombshell of this impossibility. There is a second sentence that God whispers to me in my confusion, my distress and my disappointment that alone I cannot ever be 'enough'. There is more truth to be heard:

'You are not alone.'

There is one who is 'enough'. He shines a light into the darkness of deception and unlocks freedom from the chains of our human 'enough'. His name is Jesus, and he is all you will ever need. He does not ask you to be 'enough'. He does not ask for a list of achievements, a stack of gold medals or embossed certificates; he does not require a particular body weight or a specific number of friends. He requires nothing from you except an admission that you need him, a belief that he is 'enough' and you are not. A declaration that without him, you are for ever drowning in the sea of comparison and inadequacy.

He makes you 'enough'.

I don't really understand it, if I'm completely honest. As much as I would like to, I cannot explain in simple terms the exchange that takes place when you cast yourself and all your inadequacies, your insecurities, your failures and your broken dreams at the feet of Jesus, and look only to his mercy and his grace. I cannot give you a quick, clear explanation of these love-filled intricacies.

I don't really understand it, but I can tell you of the freedom that it brings. There is such freedom to be found in letting go of 'enough' and clinging instead to Jesus, his cross and his resurrection. It seems strange that the moment you stop looking for 'enough', the moment you lay down that burden and seek first the kingdom of God, is the moment you find yourself made 'enough'. Through no effort of your own, but instead in an admission of your failure and inadequacy, you find yourself made 'enough' by the Son of God.

Suddenly, in the eyes of God, the creator of the universe, the king of all that has been made, you are 'enough'. Never before have you been, as you tried to earn your way into his favour. Never before have you reached this place of intimacy and hope, of grace, forgiveness and mercy. It is only through setting down your aspirations, your desires and your working for 'enough' that you find true freedom in the one who gave it all so that you could know love, know truth and know him.

So, as I sit here in my kitchen, writing these words with a cup of tea in my hand and my dog by my side, plagued by the age-old fear of never being 'enough', I can declare over the lies the deep truth of the love of God, and the inexpressible mystery of how he has made me 'enough'. Through Jesus' sacrifice, through the faith inspired within me by the Holy Spirit, and through God's grace and forgiveness, I am declared to be 'enough', and I can know truly, deeply and irrevocably that I am loved.

Wherever you are sitting, standing, kneeling or lying right now, know this: he calls you loved and he makes you 'enough'. There is no need to feel inadequate in the face of all that surrounds you when the king of the universe, the creator of everything seen and unseen, calls you loved and declares you—by the blood of his Son, his very self—to be 'enough'.

Speak that truth over the lies, shout it into the darkness, and bring its light to the very depths of your troubled mind. Use that truth as the key to unlock the chains of insecurity, inadequacy and failure. Know that you are loved, you are 'enough', because the Lord of all declares it over you, and nothing you ever say or do can change that.

I'm praying for you.

Love, Nell x

Musings

Welcome to my musings.

I know you're not supposed to have favourite parts of your first published work, but, between us, this is my favourite. I've loved putting this bit together most of all, and I've loved how God has spoken to me as I've written these pieces over the past few years.

In some ways, though, it's also the scariest bit.

This is the part where I'm not quietly laughing at the ridiculousness of growing up in ministry, and I'm not trying to help you think through some difficulties, addressing particular situations with gentle words and quiet suggestions.

This is the bit where I let you in. This section invites you into some of my most intimate moments with God, when I've come to him with my pain and hurt, my excitement and joy, and I've let him speak words of truth to me.

This is my faith journey—a part of it, at least. It's a journey, and I have no doubt that a year, five years, ten years from now, I'll look back and marvel at how far I have come, and how much I've changed. This faith journey is still going on, step by step, as I walk this path with Jesus by my side.

This is the most obviously theological part of the book. It's not complicated, long-winded, big-worded theology, but intimate, personal, honest theology. These are my conversations with God, a collection of words written when I was at the end of myself and when I was on top of the world, at moments of doubt and times of triumph.

This is the good, the bad and the ugly.

This is a celebration of the love that I have found. This is where I've found God weeping with me as I weep, and dancing with me as I dance. It is full of questions and searching for answers. It is honesty and brokenness met with grace and forgiveness.

This is my deep wrestling with faith, as I try to come to terms with what it means to be me. It is a discovery of what it means to be known, loved and accepted as a daughter of the king, despite it all.

This is not perfect. It is messy and broken, human and flawed.

This is not faith kept in a box and tied up with a neat little bow. It is faith lived with, lived in, questioned and doubted; faith discovered, rejoiced with, laughed with and danced with. It is truth and openness.

This is me taking passages of scripture and chewing them over, wrestling with them, sitting with them, living in them. This is me accepting God's offer of friendship and learning what it means to be loved.

This is me taking your hand and inviting you to journey with me, letting you know that you are not alone.

This is me growing into a faith of my own. Welcome to my musings.

Coming home

For when you've drifted, and you're wondering if God will welcome you back

I can't remember the last time I was here: in the silence, the stillness, the waiting, taking time to sit and be still—to remind myself of what is important and what is like snow, melting away before I can fully grasp it.

I approach, tentatively. So many weeks it has been since I was in this place. Nervously I wait. I speak into the quietness.

'Father? Are you there? I'm sorry it has been so long. I've been so busy, doing your work, helping people, honouring you in my degree, in my work, in my life… I just haven't had the time to visit. Dad, I'm sorry. But look how much I've done, Dad! Look! Dad! Dad? Are you there? Father? Where are you?'

'Child.'

One word, and peace reigns within my soul. His word, soaked in love, in adoration, soothes my troubled heart.

'Child, I have missed you,' he says quietly.

'I'm sorry, Father,' I reply, knowing full well that my excuses are poor and my apology is unjustified. 'I'm sorry, but look at…'

'No,' he says. 'No. It is not about what you have done. Your eagerness to please brings me joy, and your work has not gone unnoticed but, child, my child, I have missed your presence. Your sitting with me, chatting to me about your day, your life, your worries and your joys.

I have missed you being quiet with me. I have missed you listening to the whisper of my voice, feeling the cool breeze of my peace, the soothing balm of my love. I have missed the time we spent together every day. I am so pleased you have returned. Would you sit with me again, child? I delight in your presence.'

'Daddy,' I whisper, realising with those words how deeply I have longed for his presence. 'Daddy,' I say, 'Daddy, I've come home.' And it is there, as I collapse into his arms of grace, love and forgiveness, that I finally find what I've been looking for all along—home.

> Because you are his sons, God sent the Spirit of his Son into our hearts, the Spirit who calls out, 'Abba, Father.' So you are no longer a slave, but God's child; and since you are his child, God has made you also an heir.
>
> GALATIANS 4:6–7

Dancing in the grey

For when you're wrestling with doubt

I am a Christian, and often I do not understand. I am made continually aware of how little I understand the God I believe in and love—the God who created me, who sustains me day by day. I long to learn more about who he is and what he is like, and I struggle with not knowing.

I wrestle daily with my questions, my ignorance and my doubts. I've spent so much of my life wishing everything about God was black and white, that it made sense, that I could put it in a neat little box, tied up with a pretty little bow, and stick it on my shelf. Sometimes, I wish my God was like that. But this is not the case. That is not who God is.

There are some things of God that I know and experience to be the absolute truth. I know him to be creator, sustainer, saviour and Lord. I know him to be good, holy, pure and worthy of praise. But there are other aspects that I ponder daily, unsure of how to muddle on with so many questions. I have a large grey area of confusion and discomfort, unanswered questions and unassuaged doubt.

I do not know how God holds justice and mercy in perfect harmony. I do not know how he hates sin but loves me, a sinner. I do not know how he brings me to my knees in fear and trembling, yet invites me into his very throne room, to sit with him and call him Father. I do not know why he asks me to forgive when it still hurts, when the pain still burns deep inside. I do not know why he asks me to take the hard path and walk the narrow road. I do not know why there is suffering, and why there is pain. I do not know where he is when the darkness overwhelms and the fear surrounds, when the pain is all-encompassing and the questions lie unanswered.

For so long I have wrestled with my questions and my doubts, convinced that I cannot be a 'real' Christian if I do not have all the answers—convinced that doubt is wrong, and everything must fit together, otherwise I am foolish for believing.

But then I am approached by Jesus Christ. Jesus Christ, God incarnate, the light of the world, the Word made flesh, crucified saviour and resurrected king. He comes towards me and takes out of my hands the box of black and white in which I continually try to fit God. He takes it out of my hands, casts it aside and asks me to dance. To dance with him in the freedom that he offers and the peace that he brings in the love that spills over from his very being, and the acceptance of his leading. To dance with him in the smudges of grey that surround, confuse and disturb. But it is there, as I am accepting the invitation to dance in the grey, that truth triumphs over uncertainty. It is in the dancing that I choose first to believe, and then come to know.

I do not know how God holds justice and mercy in perfect harmony. But I know that his ways are far above mine.

I do not know how he hates sin but loves me, a sinner. But I know that I am welcomed home with open arms the moment I turn back to him.

I do not know how he brings me to my knees in fear and trembling, yet invites me into his throne room, to sit with him and call him Father. But I know that I can approach him, and he rejoices over me with singing.

I do not know why he asks me to forgive when it still hurts, when the pain still burns deep inside. But I know that every day he gives me the strength to keep going.

I do not know why he asks me to take the hard path and the narrow road. But I know that he is with me, my comforter and my protector.

I do not know why there is suffering, and why there is pain. But I know that still he is good.

I do not know where he is when the darkness overwhelms and the fear surrounds, when the pain is all-encompassing and the questions lie unanswered. But I know that still he remains.

Where the black-and-white answers are smudged into a thousand tones of grey, it is there that I will dance: in a place of uncertainty, but of peace; a place of questions, but of hope; a place of pain, but of healing; a place of frustration, but of forgiveness; a place of grey, but of dancing.

Where there are questions, where my worldview and my understanding of God are no longer black and white, no longer simple and comfortable, no longer boxed in and restricted, it is there that I will dance.

It is in the grey that I dance, but I do not dance alone. I dance a dance not of my own, but led by my saviour, my Lord and my best friend—by Jesus, by God, by the Holy Spirit. The grey of the questions does not bother me when I am in relationship with my God, because I know that he is bigger than my questions, he is trustworthy and he is faithful.

As I dance in the grey, I can embrace the questions and the doubt, the unknowns and the discomfort, and trust that he is God, he is good and he will lead me to a place of peace. Even though I do not understand, I cling to what I know to be true—that he is creator, sustainer, saviour and Lord. He is holy, pure and worthy of praise. He is faithful and he is trustworthy. He leads me step by step, even as I am dancing in the grey.

> 'For my thoughts are not your thoughts,
>   neither are your ways my ways,'
>   declares the Lord.
> 'As the heavens are higher than the earth,
>   so are my ways higher than your ways
>   and my thoughts than your thoughts.'
> ISAIAH 55:8–9

Confessions

A declaration of faith

When I tell you I'm a Christian
I'm not telling you I'm perfect.
I'm not implying that I'm better than you.
I'm saying, pure and simple, that I'm broken. Angry. Failing.
Confused. Frail. Lost. Controlling. Guarded. Chained. Anxious.
Sad. Stumbling. Insecure. Dirty. Unsure. Desolate. Ashamed.
Unworthy. Defeated. Undeserving. A sinner.

When I tell you I'm a Christian
I'm sharing with you all that I am,
all that I was,
and all that I still could be.

When I tell you I'm a Christian
I'm saying, 'Me too,'
but something more as well.

When I tell you I'm a Christian
I'm not telling you I'm perfect.
I'm not implying that I'm better than you.
I'm saying, pure and simple, that I'm broken.

Broken, but healing.
Angry, but learning to forgive.
Failing, but his grace is sufficient.
Confused, but he makes my paths straight.
Frail, but being made strong in his love.
Lost, but found in him.
Controlling, but learning to let go.

Guarded, but beginning to share.
Chained, but set free by his sacrifice.
Anxious, but laying my burdens on him.
Sad, but his mercies are new every morning.
Stumbling, but leaning on the solid rock.
Insecure, but fearfully and wonderfully made.
Dirty, but washed clean with his blood.
Unsure, but his faithfulness is great.
Desolate, but he is my comforter.
Ashamed, but there is no condemnation in him.
Unworthy, but a new creation.
Defeated, but victorious with him.
Undeserving, but showered with grace.
A sinner, in need of a saviour.

When I tell you I'm a Christian,
I'm saying that I've been shown
a better way.
A way to be which makes life worth living
and people worth loving.
A way which makes you feel more alive
than anything else.
That makes you whole in a way
you didn't think possible.
That heals scars you thought you'd carry for ever.
That shows you that you are worth more
than you could even begin to imagine.
That brings a peace that this world
can neither give
nor take away.

When I tell you I'm a Christian, you see,
I'm sharing with you my journey,
and asking you to join me
on this road of redemption.
A road paved with hope.

A road of repentance,
of trials
and tribulations,
but a road
which satisfies,
and heals.
Which comforts,
and restores.
A road
marked out
from the beginning of time
for you.
Leading
to the creator
and sustainer
of all.
Who runs,
arms wide open,
face beaming,
heart bursting,
as he sees you
begin the journey
back to where you belong.

So
will you join me
on this road?
Broken people
met by a healing saviour.
Redeemed, cleansed, restored, forgiven.
Loved.

Chains

For times when you are weighed down with
painful memories and deep hurts

I suppose there's something strangely comfortable about the chains that have bound us for many years. They are familiar. Their weight becomes a part of what we carry around each day. We know how they feel around our wrists and ankles; we know how to go about our day-to-day business with them on, restricted, but functioning.

They make up a part of us; they define us and everything that we do, and because of that, we live with them. No two people's chains are the same. For some people they are the chains of self-loathing, of never feeling good enough; for others they are the chains of others' expectations, of the burning desire to succeed but never quite managing it. Or they are the chains of the lies we have been told for years, the chains of what someone did or didn't do. Or maybe they are the weight of anxiety, the compulsive need for everything to be 'just so' but never being quite right.

These chains weigh us down, yes, but the weight becomes such an integral part of our being that we are scared to take them off. We let them define us in the way that we promised ourselves we never would. And so we live with them. We carry them around with us every day, letting them restrict us.

But one day we get tired. We see people around us who are not restricted, who don't have our chains, and we realise just how weary we really are, how much our body aches and how we drag our feet. We realise how inhibited we are, how our growth has been limited, our potential not reached.

Then we hear of the one who promises to set the captives free—not just those who are held captive by others, but also those who are held captive by themselves, who are prisoners of their insecurities, their failings and their anxieties. Not only does this man promise to set the captives free, but he declares that he has already done it. He has already unlocked the chains that bound us. We are already free, should we wish to be so.

But freedom is scary. Freedom brings with it the ability to do anything, and that potential is truly terrifying. The unknown is impossible to control, impossible to comprehend. The familiar weight of our chains is almost comforting when we are faced with the fear of the unknown. And more than that, we can't quite bring ourselves to believe that our chains really have been undone, that we really have been set free. The chains of insecurity, worthlessness and anxiety weigh us down, even as they are undone.

But while we concentrate on the dead weight around our wrists and ankles, what we forget is that the truth can, and the truth will, set us free. If only we were to raise our eyes from the ground, we would see a man hanging on a cross, asking for our chains, telling us he loves us. Telling us we're worth it. Telling us not to worry because he's got it under control. Telling us the truth. And if we do raise our eyes from the ground, if we do stop to listen, just for a moment; if we do take a deep breath and, in faith, shake off those chains that have bound us for so very long; if we do listen to the truth and choose to believe it, then it really will set us free.

> [Jesus] said to her, 'Daughter, your faith has healed you. Go in peace and be freed from your suffering.'
> MARK 5:34

Walking the forgiveness path

For when you need to understand forgiveness, again

I'm beginning to learn that forgiveness is not an option, but it is a choice. No one can force you into forgiveness; it's not real forgiveness if you feel that you have to do it for one reason or another. It's a choice that has to be freely made because you want to, because you need to, because you know that, until you do, you will never truly be free.

Forgiveness is scary. It feels like giving up, like saying that what that person did to you, to those you love, was OK. But it's not. Forgiveness is being brave. It is having the courage to let go; to unfurl the fist in which you've grasped the anger, the hurt, the resentment, the hatred and the tears for so long, and to hand it over; to relinquish your desire for revenge, your desire for them to know just how much they've hurt you. It is placing that person at the foot of the cross and trusting God with them.

Forgiveness is saying to that person, 'Yes, you hurt me. Yes, it still hurts me now. Yes, sometimes I want to scream and yell and cry and hurt you just as much as you hurt me, but actually I'm not going to let you hurt me any more. You have no right to be my burden. I refuse to carry you around with me, and I refuse to let my anger towards you define me any longer. I am letting it go. I am taking a deep breath, closing my eyes and cutting the cords that bind you to me. I know what you did; I acknowledge that you have hurt me and those whom I love more than I can begin to express, but I'm surrendering my right to revenge. I'm handing you over to the one who knows all, and I trust him to treat you fairly, because my anger and my humanity cannot, because I know that my hurting you will not solve anything. Hurting you, getting my own back, seeking revenge, will not remove any of the pain you caused me. But that does not matter, because no longer are you a part of what I carry, and no longer can you hurt me.'

The path to forgiveness is not an easy one, but it is the only one that sets you free. The other paths may seem far easier, far safer and far more comfortable, but, a few miles down those paths, the weight that you carry on your back becomes too much. That person who has hurt you, whom you have been carrying around for years upon years, clings on ever tighter until you do not have the strength to go on. You are consumed by their weight and by the pain that they have caused you. Your whole world is affected by the burden you carry with you, by the anger that, somewhere along the way, you allowed to define you.

The path to forgiveness starts with a leap, as you cross the chasm between the easy path and the hard one. It is an uphill struggle, day by day, a choice to put one foot in front of the other. For a while, on the forgiveness path, you still carry that burden, the heavy weight on your back, because you're still too scared to let it go. But although the forgiveness path is darker, rougher and harder, you do not walk it alone. On the forgiveness path, you have a rod and a staff, you have a light and you have a companion.

On the forgiveness path, you have Jesus. He walks beside you, guiding your way and steadying you when you stumble. Step by step, he not only holds your hand, but, little by little, he takes away your burden. He takes the weight off your shoulders, bit by bit, until one day you are free. And when you reach the end of the forgiveness path, he is the one who takes you in his arms, shows you the view and says, 'Look how far we've come. My child, I am so very proud of you.'

> Therefore, as God's chosen people, holy and dearly loved, clothe yourselves with compassion, kindness, humility, gentleness and patience. Bear with each other and forgive one another if any of you has a grievance against someone. Forgive as the Lord forgave you.
> COLOSSIANS 3:12–13

Interrupted

For when you are angry at God

I am raging. Seething. Furious. Anger pulsates through my bones, through my very being. It's a deep-seated, overwhelming, red-hot anger that I cannot articulate and cannot control. It's anger at how life has turned out—what has happened, what has been done, what has been said. It's anger at what has *not* happened, what has not been done, what has *not* been said. I say that I am angry at other people, at the situation, at the world. But really, truly, honestly, I am angry at you.

I am a child having a tantrum. I am stamping my feet and throwing my breakfast cereal at the wall. I am fists-clenched, eyes-closed, throat-raw, nose-streamingly angry. I am red-faced, indignant. I am helpless and hopeless, inconsolable and singled-minded in my rage. I have been screaming and wailing for so long that I can't remember why I'm angry; all I know is that it hurts. I am trying to deflect it, to direct it at something, someone, anyone else. But really, truly, honestly, I am angry at you.

I am self-absorbed, so engrossed in my life that I am blind to the pain of others. I am lashing out, wounding, inflicting pain on those closest to me. I am battling with anger and rage, confusion and fear. I am scared and lonely. I am disgruntled and sceptical, angry and selfish. I am unstoppable in my anger, strong in my hurt, blind to my actions. I am the best of the best and the worst of the worst. I am powerful and I am vulnerable. I am fierce and I am scared. I am angry at that which I cannot change, at that which will form me. I project my anger on to all that surrounds me, but really, truly, honestly, I am angry at you.

It feels as if I am forgotten, like a child, lost in a supermarket; a traveller, alone in a foreign land; a stray animal, abandoned. I feel alone, forgotten, unloved and unwanted.

Why do you not hear me? Why do you not care? Where have you been? Where did you go? You promised that you would be there, but I cannot feel you any more. Why have you left me? Why did you let it happen? Why do I not understand? You said that I mattered, and yet I feel as if I have been left by the wayside to find my own way home.

I say that I am angry at a situation, a word, an action, a life development. I say that I am angry at anything other than what I am really angry at, because really, truly, honestly, I am angry at you.

I stand in front of you, nose to nose, fists clenched, yelling and screaming in rage and disappointment, and you interrupt me.

You interrupt me.

You interrupt me with love.

It's not an action I can describe, not something a word can explain. It comes as soft as a breath, quieter than a whisper, and yet my anger is no match for its strength, its surety, its truth. It is inexplicable and impossible to articulate, but it is undeniable in its power and its steadfast hope. It is the one thing I never expected. It is the reaction that defuses the ticking time bomb of my heart.

You interrupt me.

You interrupt me with love.

I do not know how this story ends. I do not know if the anger has truly gone, eclipsed in the light of your love. The anger is deep, and I fear that it will soon fight its way back to the surface, exploding out of me with crass words and dark thoughts. I do not know where this path will lead, but for now I will dwell here. I will sit in the moment when my anger is pushed aside by the interruption of your love.

The anger runs deep, but in this interruption there dwells a deeper truth. Deeper than the rage, the anger, the seething and the fury, there is truth—it's the truth of the love that you offer. A truth that I am not alone, and I never was, for you have promised never to leave me or forsake me. The truth that you never promised life would be easy, and I was wrong to expect it to be so. The truth that there is no need to be afraid, for this perfect love casts out fear. The truth which asks me to place you at the centre, with the reassurance that surrender leads to new life. The truth that things may not change but your grace is sufficient. The truth that I am weak but you are strong. The truth that even the darkness cannot blot out this light. The truth that even the weight of lies cannot overwhelm.

I do not know where we go from here. I do not know where the anger has retreated to or where it is hiding. I do not know if this interruption of love will become a sentence, a paragraph, a page, a chapter, a book or a library. I do not know how the story ends. All I know is that, for now, I must pause at the interruption. For now, I must dwell in the breath that you give me when you interrupt my raging with a word. For now, I trust you with my anger, for I know that you—and only you—can cope with it, deal with it and neutralise it. You are the only one it will not overwhelm. You, the one who calmed the wind and the waves with a word, can calm my anger with an interruption. For now, at least, my anger no longer has a hold on me, for as you interrupted it, you stole its power over me.

I was angry, but you interrupted me.

You interrupted me with love.

> [Jesus] got up, rebuked the wind and said to the waves, 'Quiet! Be still!' Then the wind died down and it was completely calm.
> MARK 4:39

Trust and obey

For when you're struggling with what God has asked of you

Have you ever been scared? Have you ever been truly afraid? Have you ever been terrified? Have you ever been unsure of which way to go next? Have you ever felt as if you were stumbling around in the pitch blackness, in a place full of obstacles that are there to hurt you? Maybe you've been faced with a room full of people shouting at you, throwing accusations at you, blaming you for things that are not your fault. Or perhaps it's just the overwhelming feeling that all hope is lost, that it will never get better, that this is all life is and all it will ever be. That feeling scares you and you don't know what to do.

When fear confronts us, the world tells us we have two choices: fight or flight. Raise your fists and your voice and make sure that you are protected in every way you possibly can be. Fight fire with fire. Shout louder. Do not back down. Keep going until the bitter end. Or run away. Leave before it gets too messy; before you get hurt; before your family gets hurt; before you lose something important, like your home or your money or your life.

When fear confronts us, the world tells us we have two choices. But God tells us we have three: fight, or flight, or trust and obey.

Trust that 'in all things God works for the good of those who love him' (Romans 8:28). Trust that when you are bedridden and unable to move, God will use you to speak in other ways. Trust that when you are two months away from losing your job, your house and your income, and it seems that all your bridges have been burnt, God will carry you across the raging waters that surround you. Trust that when your daughter is one month into her GCSE year and still doesn't have a school place, God will give her something better than you could ever ask for or imagine. Trust that even though it hurts and it's confusing and you just want out, God knows what he's doing. Trust that when it is so dark and so scary and so dangerous that you are too frightened even to move, God will take your hand and guide you through it all and out the other side. Trust that 'when you walk through the fire, you will not be burned' (Isaiah 43:2). Trust that when you do not have the strength to forgive, and you're scared of letting go, God will show you how to love and give you peace. Trust that even though you cannot see the sun behind the clouds, it's still shining.

Trust and obey.

Obey God's call to stick at it just a little longer. Obey his command not to be afraid, for he is 'with you always, to the very end of the age' (Matthew 28:20). Obey his call 'to act justly and to love mercy and to walk humbly with him' (Micah 6:8). Obey him when he asks the hardest things of you—to 'love your enemies and pray for those who persecute you' (Matthew 5:44). Trust that when you reach your human limitations, when you cannot do it any more, when the burden becomes too much, and the frustration is too great, and the anger is destroying you, trust that he will give you exactly what you need. Trust that he will take the burden from you and give you the love you need, the strength to forgive and the peace that you so long for.

Trust and obey.

When fear confronts us, we have a choice. We can run. We can fight. Or we can trust. We can ignore our problems and bury our heads in the sand, or leave and never look back, turn tail and run. We can fight, risking pain and anguish and hurt and disaster. Or we can stand quietly, stop for a minute and listen—not to the pounding of the blood in our ears, not to the voices shouting accusations, not to the silence that tells us all hope is lost, not to the lies that say nothing will ever get better, but to the still small voice, belonging to the one who climbs into the boat in the middle of the raging lake and says to us, 'Take courage! It is I. Don't be afraid' (Matthew 14:27).

Only when we stand quietly and listen for that still small voice, only then do we recognise our true human weakness and see Christ's strength made perfect through it. When we run, we run not only from the fear but also from the hope. When we fight, we ignore the peace which is offered to us. But when we trust and obey, it is then that we find the answer. We find the peace. We find the truth. We find the hope. And we find the freedom—from violence, lies, anger, unforgiveness, worry and fear. By the grace of God and in his strength, all we have to do is trust and obey.

Trust in the Lord with all your heart
    and lean not on your own understanding;
in all your ways submit to him,
    and he will make your paths straight.
PROVERBS 3:5–6

Hide-and-seek

For when you are hiding but long to be found

Hide-and-seek: hands covering eyes. If I can't see you, you can't see me. Peek-a-boo, there you are. Childlike laughter wafts above the drone of adult conversation that surrounds me. These are the games we play, that keep a child entertained for hours at a time— simple hiding, joyful seeking. The fun is unending, the laughter unquenchable.

Hide-and-seek: a childish game. Crouched in a cupboard or curled up behind a curtain, I am hiding from the seeker, from my parents, from a friend. Hiding—but not very well. A giggle escapes my lips, rising out above the shelter in which I have enclosed myself, revealing my whereabouts to those pretending not to notice.

Hide-and-seek: a bit of fun. I am running away as you cover your face and eyes to count to 20. I am manically dashing from place to place, looking for an area big enough to hold my small frame. I become ensconced in a tiny opening and settle down for the long haul, determined, this time, to keep the secret of the space in which I have chosen to dwell. But I am too transparent; my hiding places are too obvious. You find me, every time, with joy in your eyes and triumph on your face. You pick me up and place me on your shoulders, walking back home with a spring in your step. You have sought me and I have been found.

Hide-and-seek: I'm getting better now. No longer do I fit in the small places; the physical constraints of my frame are harder to overcome. But this is a physical game no more. This is another level, a new dimension. No longer do I hide crouched in a cupboard or curled up behind a curtain. Now I hide from you within myself. Walls up, door closed, I hide behind fear, excuses, lies. They clothe me and conceal my deepest desires, my longing for freedom.

Hide-and-seek: you won't find me now. I am determined to be hidden. Refusing to be seen, I curl up tightly, ashamed and alone, scared of what you will find if you seek me. I curl around my shame as it cloaks my very being. I retreat into the depths of my anger, fighting off any suggestion of peace. I wander into the darkness of unforgiveness, rejecting the light of grace which I know you will bring.

Hide-and-seek: I am scared. In hiding from you, I have lost myself. It is dark and my burden is heavy but I am proud. I remain, hiding in plain sight, positioned in a place that people know but do not see. Never do they find me. Never do they look to see who I truly am. The lies, they hide me. The shame, it chokes me. The fear, it paralyses me. Because I am hidden in plain sight, no one knows the war that rages behind the smile, the secret darkness in the corners of my mind.

Hide-and-seek: I don't know what to do. A childhood game has become an adult nightmare, and I am trapped. I am trapped in the darkness, in the lies and in the fear. Unable to escape, I am barred by that which I have been hiding for so long. The thoughts that I have been concealing, the secret depths of my soul, the darkness, the instincts, the confusion, the lies, the pain—they have turned on me and suddenly they overwhelm me. I am trapped and I cannot escape. Helpless and hopeless, I hide away.

Hide-and-seek: I am all alone. Hiding is a lonely game. Trapped in the hiddenness, I cannot see a way out. Crying out for freedom, I remain hidden by the depths, in the corner, in the fortress of my past, my fears and my loneliness. I think you have forgotten me, trapped and scared as I am by the fortress of my mind. It has been so long since you heard me, I decide you must have given up, gone home and left me to my brokenness and my hiding.

Hide-and-seek: yet you come. Your soft footsteps are approaching. There's a quiet knock at the door of my heart. I hold my breath; maybe you won't hear the inhaling and exhaling that threaten to give away my presence. Ashamed and alone, a battle rages. I do not want to be found; I fear what you will see and know when you find me; and yet all I long for is to be discovered by you.

Hide-and-seek: I can hear you now. Calling my name, your voice is warm and gentle, your tone accepting and calm. Closer and closer, you are seeking and searching, persistent with your calling as you stand at the door of my mind, my heart, my soul. You know that I am in there, and you long for me to come out. But I am ashamed, I am scared and I am alone. I do not know if you will want me when you see who I truly am.

Hide-and-seek: you speak truth. Standing close to my hiding place, you whisper light into my darkness. You tell me gently, in words that only I can hear, of how you love me, how you know me fully and accept me in all of my brokenness. Drawing ever closer, you speak truth over the lies, bring peace to the fear.

Hide-and-seek: I begin to whisper. I whisper to you of what I am ashamed. I tell you of the fear; I share with you my darkness. I whisper words of regret and deep repentance, and I throw myself on your mercy. I cry out to you with my pain, I repent of my failings and I find myself met with grace.

Hide-and-seek: you draw me out. Bit by bit, word by word, line by line, you bring me closer to you. As you speak, as you whisper truth, you tell me who I am. You speak words of light and love, peace and hope, grace and forgiveness. You tell me of your sacrifice for me, how you gave your very being so that I could be free, so that I could be found. You share your longing to be with me, to laugh with me, to rejoice with me once again. You invite me into your plans for me, your joy at our partnership. You weep over my pain and you soothe me with the gentle balm of your love.

Hide-and-seek: no longer am I hiding. I have been found in the truth of who you say that I am. I have been found and brought out into the light, redeemed and restored in the confession of all that I was hiding. Now I am hidden with Christ in you, in the shadow of your wings, and it is here that I find who I truly am. Forgiven, loved, accepted and found—I am fully yours.

> Whoever dwells in the shelter of the Most High
>   will rest in the shadow of the Almighty.
> I will say of the Lord, 'He is my refuge and my fortress,
>   my God, in whom I trust.'
>
> PSALM 91:1–2

Be still

For when the noise and demands of the world are overwhelming

Peace and quiet. Time to sit, time to relax, time to reflect. Everyone longs for that moment at the end of a long day when they can sit down, kick off their shoes and just be. And yet we never just 'are'. There is always something to do, something to think about, something to worry about, something to distract us from just being. Our world never really stops. Our brains never really quieten. Our bodies are never really still. We fill our lives with things to keep us occupied, things to watch, things to read, things to do. There's always 'one more thing' to complete before we can relax. There's always one more person to satisfy before we ourselves can be satisfied. There's always one more item we need to check off our to-do list before we feel in control enough to relax. We're never truly fulfilled. Our minds are continually on what needs to be done tomorrow, worrying about a deadline, fretting about that unfinished business, that incomplete plan, that piece of our life that is not yet under control.

We burden ourselves by believing that we can never truly be still, never really have peace, unless everything is sorted, unless life is in control, unless the plan is complete. We burden ourselves by believing a lie. We are deceived into carrying a burden that is not ours to bear, a load that is not our responsibility to shoulder. It's a heavy weight draped around our very being, an ever-present part of who we are, a defining piece of us, something that makes us feel useful, needed, wanted, loved.

We are in control, but not relaxed—never relaxed, never peaceful and certainly never still. We are always longing for peace and quiet, for that moment when our thoughts are silent and our heart is no longer heavy. We are always longing for something that we can never have unless we let go and relinquish control, unless we acknowledge that maybe, just maybe, we don't know best. Maybe, just maybe, our plan is flawed. Maybe, just maybe, someone else knows better.

But acknowledging this would be to acknowledge our failings, to acknowledge that we don't have it all sussed. We don't know what we're doing or where we're going, and sometimes, sometimes we don't even know who we are any more. For so long we've placed our identity in our ability to have everything sorted, to be the one who has their life under control. And to acknowledge that we don't—well, that would mean losing a part of who we are.

But maybe in that loss we will gain something greater. In that loss we will gain a certain type of peace—a peace that passes all understanding; a peace that says we don't have to be in control any more, because someone else has a handle on it—someone far bigger, far more reliable and far better at it than we ever could be: God. The God who created the world, set the planets in motion and holds the universe in the palm of his hand—the God who knows us better than we know ourselves—is in control. He is in control so that we don't have to be.

With that realisation, that relinquishing of control, comes something of which we had only ever dreamed. With that knowledge comes peace and quiet: a quiet brain, a still body, a peaceful heart. There is silence, an ability to be—to not worry, not think, not do anything, just to be still and know that he is God.

> He says, 'Be still, and know that I am God;
>   I will be exalted among the nations,
>   I will be exalted in the earth.'
> PSALM 46:10

Barefoot

A spiritual reflection on John 13

What does it mean to be barefoot? There are no shoes for protection, no socks for warmth. Feet are exposed to the elements, at the mercy of the weather and the terrain that surrounds. There is a suggestion of safety, yet a feeling of being free.

Barefoot is trust, risk, a game. Barefoot feels like home, a secure place to dwell. Barefoot is intimacy and exposure. Barefoot is vulnerability, openness, an opportunity to be hurt. Barefoot is painful from the texture of the road beneath my feet and the gravel under my toes, sticking into my skin.

Barefoot is warm grass tickling my arches, sand crunching between my toes. Barefoot is mud-squelching, water-running freedom. Barefoot is summer holidays spent by the sea, running in and out of the waves, skimming stones and chasing the wind. Barefoot is the kitchen floor, knees to chest, face down, tears falling. Barefoot is sitting in the long grass, picking daisies with my toes.

Barefoot tells stories of roads walked, water swum in, trees climbed. Barefoot speaks of the places I've been that no one else knows, the times spent running from life and from love, the moments spent racing towards far-flung hopes and dreams.

Barefoot is dirty and grimy, dusty and worn. Barefoot is smelly and broken and not at my best. Barefoot shows the journey; it keeps no secrets and covers no scars. Barefoot speaks of places of intimacy and places of pain. Barefoot is broken shoes, sore feet, bleeding toes. Barefoot is memories, stories, reminders.

Barefoot is where you find me. Barefoot is how you love me.

Bare feet in a basin filled with water. Bare feet, with a towel wrapped around your waist. Bare feet, as you kneel before me—leader, servant, friend. Bare feet, as clear, fresh, cool water comes tumbling down over my toes, my ankles, my arches. Bare feet, for if you do not wash me I have no part in you. Bare feet, and it is you with whom I long to dwell.

Bare feet, lovingly washed by hands not my own. Bare feet, toes curling in embarrassment, gently caressed, adored and loved until they relax under your touch. Bare feet, with the memories of countless steps walked, countless paths trodden, unending terrains covered. Bare feet, the reminder of laughter and of tears, of trouble and of pain.

Bare feet, with the grime and the grit of the places I have travelled etched into their very soles. Bare feet, a reflection of the grime and grit of my life, my being, my experiences, my pain and my mess.

Bare feet, washed clean by the creator of the universe. Bare feet, adored by the saviour of the world. Bare feet, seen by the one who sees it all, touched by the one who formed the earth. Bare feet, caressed by the hands that flung stars into space.

Bare feet. At my worst and at my best, it is here that you find me. It is here that you see me, know me, love me. It is here that you cleanse me, and it is here that I am home.

> [Jesus] poured water into a basin and began to wash his disciples' feet, drying them with the towel that was wrapped round him.
> JOHN 13:5

Battling

For when the darkness feels too much to bear

It is dark. A heavy darkness. The kind that presses in on you and makes it hard to breathe. A dark that surrounds and engulfs you, and makes you forget that anything good ever existed. A dark that terrifies and blinds. This seemingly unending darkness changes words and thoughts and actions. It recreates battles you thought had been won long ago. It brings back memories you thought you had forgotten. It reminds you of hurts you believed you had forgiven.

It is silent, too. Silence is golden, or so the saying goes. Silence is golden, but the air shimmers like the summer heat with unspoken words, undisclosed secrets and unfriendly memories. The silence says it all. Silence really does speak louder than words. The silence yells abuse, whispers compliments and ties everything up in knots until there is nothing left to say any more. Silence can bring the world to its feet or send it crashing down around you.

But silence is deafening; it always has been. A million voices longing for you to believe a million lies all speak through the silence, dictating your next words and making you forget all that will follow. Silence reveals the deepest insecurities of your heart in a way that words never could. And silence—you knew—would be your downfall. Silence is beginning to defeat you, but you will not go down without a fight.

'His gr...' You clear your throat. These words are important, but, as you speak, the darkness grows heavier and the silence grows louder, overwhelming your thoughts and intercepting your words. You are fighting back the darkness, and you have only these few short words.

'His grace is sufficient.' A break in the silence. 'And his power…' It is too much: the darkness is getting heavier, overwhelming and overtaking you. But you have to speak. The only way to get rid of the darkness is to bring in the light. You try again.

'His grace is sufficient. And his power is made perfect in weakness.' As the words are released into the silence, something breaks through the darkness. It is a light—dim at first, but growing brighter with every word. You look around you but the light is not there. And yet the darkness is retreating. You glance down. The light is coming from inside of you. It is radiating its bright yellow-white rays from your heart. And as you speak words of truth, it glows brighter still.

'There is now no condemnation for those who are in Christ Jesus.' The light burns brighter.

'In all things God works for the good of those who love him.' The darkness is retreating.

'He who began a good work in me will carry it on to completion.' The heaviness is dissipating.

'I can do all this through Christ who gives me strength.' The air clears.

'The one who is in me is greater than the one who is in the world.' The light bursts forth from within you, and suddenly there is no longer any darkness. You are bathed in glorious light. Radiating from within, it is shining its truth over you, eclipsing the darkness which had threatened to overwhelm. You are free from the heaviness, the oppression, the battles, the lies, the hurt. The light has overcome what you could not.

> The light shines in the darkness, and the darkness has not overcome it.
> JOHN 1:5

Fingertip faith

A cry for help

When the trials of this world buffet me
and despair is close at hand;
when betrayal, lies and fear
clothe my every move, my every waking thought,
I will cry to you, O my God.

When the wind is strong and the waves roar beneath me,
I will cling to 'the rock that is higher than I'.
When darkness surrounds and emptiness overwhelms me,
by my fingertips I will cling.

For I know that you are good,
and your love endures for ever.
I know your hand guides me, your grace sustains me and
your faithfulness is never-ending.
Teach me again of your love, O Lord.
Show me once more how it changes and calms,
ends striving and gives freely;
how it gently heals and renews, comforts and adores.

These fingertips of faith remind me of your promises;
they teach me your truth,
whisper hope in the darkness
and hold on when all else seems lost.
When doubts shout louder than hope in my mind
I will trust in you, O my saviour.
When you ask me to trust in your power alone,
and control chokes the 'yes' in my throat,
I will throw myself once again on to your grace.

For I know you have mercy that reaches
deeper even than my failings;
grace never ending, peace that surpasses all.
I know your loving guidance in the midst of the battle, and
that your victory is mine through the blood of the Lamb.

But Lord, I am scared, I am weak and I am poor.
I have nothing but these fingertips of faith.
Father, would you teach me?
Jesus, would you guide me?
Spirit, would you comfort me?
Give me faith in the day, and perseverance in the night.
Give me strength to forgive, love to sustain, patience to
endure.

Father, I am nothing without this rock to which I cling.
Without you I am empty, lost and broken.
Apart from you my words are meaningless,
and all my hope is in vain.

But I know that you are with me.
I trust in your promises, and I know your word to be true.
Equip me for battle; give me faith where I am lacking.
Teach me to trust you,
give me joy and give me peace.

How much longer until these fingertips grow stronger?
When will I learn to grasp your truth and your peace?
Lord, I am lacking, scared and unsure;
my heart grows fainter and my grip gets weaker,
so I ask you to strengthen these fingertips of faith.

From the ends of the earth I call to you,
    I call as my heart grows faint;
    lead me to the rock that is higher than I.
PSALM 61:2

I prayed for a friend

For those who walk the journey with us

A year after moving to a new city, sitting quietly after school one day, it felt strange to pray—quite simply—for a friend.

I prayed for a friend, and God gave me you. You, with your love of singing and your strange cereal habits. You, with your voice that sounds like velvet feels. You, with your half-smile that begins on the left side of your mouth and grows to slowly encompass your whole face. You, the one with the evasive half-answers and an ability to gently ask the questions I don't really want to think about. You, and your sitting with me through the questions and the wrestling, the triumphs and the trials. You, with your giggle and your pedantic knowledge of niche grammatical rules. You, with your half cups of tea, your capacity to listen and your way of somehow making everyone feel truly loved and deeply valued, no matter what.

Sitting on a train, on my way back to university for a second term, I was beginning to get used to it, but still the words were stilted and shy as I prayed—once again—for a friend.

I prayed for a friend, and God gave me you. You, with your incredible passion and your irresistible enthusiasm. You, with your integrity and your stubborn persistence. You, with kindness and gentleness in your words and in your actions. You, with your broad shoulders and lively mind. You, with your hair that never quite sits flat and your strange love of charity-shop jumpers. You, the one who dreamed big and never gave up. You, with your kind dark eyes and your infectious laugh. You, with your impressions and your childish sense of humour. You, with your desire for secondhand books and your ability to listen. You, with your humility and your bold prayers, your joy and your grace.

I didn't know what would happen when I prayed, again, for a friend. But there was still more to learn.

I prayed for a friend, and God gave me you. You, with your wild hair and your dry sense of humour. You, with your unswerving faithfulness and abundant generosity. You, with your sass and your love of rationality. You, with your kindness and your willingness to always go the extra mile. You, with your honesty, your compassion and your desire to make a real difference. You, with your fierce independence and your raised eyebrow, your eye roll and your dad jokes. You, the one who never fails to keep a promise and never says no to a good old-fashioned G&T. You, with your capacity for organisation and your humble acceptance of (written) compliments.

Once again, I came to God, and I asked him for another friend. Not because I was lacking, but because I knew there was more of himself he wished to teach me.

I prayed for a friend, and God gave me you. Sitting in a park on a sunny July afternoon, a lunchtime picnic became an afternoon discussion as we chased the sunshine across the sky, moving around the grass to keep the warmth on our faces. You, with your enthusiasm and your childlike joy. You, with your unending encouragement and your solid presence. You, with your eyes-closed-thinking face. You, with your love of puns and strange fascination with pictures of explosions. You, with your sense of adventure and desire to climb trees. You, with your never-ending search for understanding and your deep love of Jesus. You, the one who sits on my kitchen floor with me, because I once mentioned that it made me feel at home.

Down the years, I have asked God for a friend. One by one, friends have come. Some have stayed, others have been called elsewhere. But they have never failed to teach me something new—about friendship, about love, about God. Time after time, God has given me someone truly remarkable to do life with for a little while, and, through them, he has given me himself. In friend after friend after friend, he has shown me a part of who he is and, through their love, he has shown me a small reflection of his abounding love for me.

I prayed for a friend, and God gave me himself. God, sitting with me through the questions and the wrestling, the triumphs and the trials. God, with kindness and gentleness in his words and in his actions. God, with his unswerving faithfulness and abundant generosity. God, with his unending encouragement and his solid presence. God, who cannot be fully described with words but must be discovered through searching and seeking, knocking and asking. God, who knows my prayers before the words have left my lips, whose love is not possessive or jealous but who knows me completely and slowly teaches me to become who he made me to be. God, who saw that it was not good for me to be alone, and so gave me friends to teach me something of himself. God who is, in his very being, community and fellowship. God, who died and rose again so that I could know freedom, so that I could know truth and so that I could know him.

I thank my God every time I remember you.
PHILIPPIANS 1:3

Here is love

For when love hurts

It seems so easy to sing some old hymns or the modern worship songs... the tunes roll off your tongue and you so often forget to pay attention to the words you are belting out at the top of your lungs.

And yet, when you stop to listen to what you are singing, it can really hit you, right in the gut. You realise that if God took you at your word (or your song), you might well find yourself in quite an unexpected and difficult situation. This struck me very clearly a few years back, as I sang 'Hosanna' by Hillsong United. One line in particular got to me: 'Show me how to love like you have loved me.'

The thing is, though, no one tells you how hard it is to love—to really love, to really care, to really feel; to care so deeply, utterly, completely and totally about someone that you don't have the words for it any more. This is not love as the world tells it; this is not erotic love or platonic love; this is a love that does not come from a human heart. This is a love that comes from Love himself—from God himself.

But this love—this deep, honest, raw, painful love—hurts. It's hard. It hurts to see someone you love in pain, in turmoil, in confusion. It hurts to see them bound by lies and false beliefs and anger and memories and unforgiveness. It hurts to see someone you care for so deeply believing lies about themselves, hurting themselves, hating themselves, putting themselves down, denying themselves, running away from themselves and never truly looking at themselves, because they're scared of what they might see.

Love hurts. Real love is painful. It moves you to tears. It moves you to sighs and 'groanings too deep for words' (Romans 8:26, ESV). It moves you to a prayer and a cry so deep, you don't know what you're asking for, but you know that it's needed. But this love—this painful, deep, honest love—comes as a shock. Love isn't meant to be painful, you say. Love is supposed to be fluffy and warm and fuzzy. But love was never easy. Look to the cross. Look to the ultimate expression of love, to Love himself dying on a cross out of love for you.

And this, this is the love that God calls us to have. This bloodied, beaten, torn-down, humiliated, unspeakable, painful, beautiful love for others is the love that God gives us when we ask for it. When we ask God to 'show me how to love like you have loved me', he may well give us what we ask for. Not a love for every single person—no one human being can bear that burden; God bears it for us—but maybe just for a particular group of people: the lost, the broken, the widows, the orphans, the survivors, the victims, the perpetrators, the prisoners, the hungry, the sick, the mentally ill, the dying, the lonely…

Or maybe God will give you love just for one person, just that one person who everyone finds it so hard to understand, but who you cannot help but love—that one broken, hurting, lost, scared person who needs God's love more than you could ever know. God may call you to show them that love. Imagine what a difference we could make in the world if we were each able to love just one person like this—to see one person as God sees them, and love them with a mere fraction of the love that God has for them.

Never will we be able to fully understand the depth of God's love for us and for those around us, but the moment when we begin to love someone in that deep, painful, God-given way is the moment that we take one step closer to understanding God's extraordinary, incomparable love for them and, in turn, for us as well.

If you feel that this love is tearing you apart, that it's too much for you to bear, look again to the cross. Look to Love, dying on the cross. Know that his power is made perfect in weakness and that he loves you with an everlasting love. Even at those moments when it feels as if someone's life depends on you loving them, taking care of them and supporting them—when it feels as if you're holding their life in your hands—remember that 'underneath are the everlasting arms' and those arms will never fail.

Don't forget that the God with these everlasting arms loves that person even more than you do. He has the capacity to love them more than you can ever imagine. Even though it might hurt to let them go, even though it may feel as if you are dropping them into the unknown, just know that the hands that are holding yours, even as you are holding them, are strong and mighty to save, and they truly will never fail.

Do not be afraid of this love, this deep, honest love. There is no fear in love. It hurts, but it's worth it. As someone once said bitterly to me, 'Pain is the price you pay for caring.' 'Yes,' I responded, 'but it's worth it every single time.' One day, God willing, you will see the result of this small amount of 'God-love' that you have shown. You will see the day when the butterfly unfurls from the cocoon, when the flower finally opens its petals and turns, in full beauty, towards the one who made it. He is the one who will then make it whole with his perfect, complete, deep, honest, painful, all-consuming, never-changing, eternal love.

Real love hurts. Real love is not easy. Real love comes from God, the one who is wholly love. But peace comes from God too, as do strength and refuge. Do not be afraid to ask God for his love for someone, but do not do so lightly. Love is a burden, but it is also freedom. The freedom that comes with loving someone, or with being loved by someone, cannot be explained or written off. It is scary, and it is hard, and it hurts, but do not be afraid of it. Perfect love—real love, God's love, God himself—casts out fear. So fear not, for he is with you, especially as you love. After all, we love because he first loved us.

> This is how we know what love is: Jesus Christ laid down his life for us. And we ought to lay down our lives for our brothers and sisters.
> 1 JOHN 3:16

On being human

For when you feel ill-equipped to tackle life's difficulties

There's something I have to tell you, something I think you need to know. I don't really know how to say it, but it's important that you hear it. It's going to hurt, and it's going to turn your world upside down. But I promise you, it will make things better. People have been telling you the opposite for years upon years, but it's time someone told you the truth. And so, here it is.

You are not superhuman.

Actually, no. Stop. I won't let myself talk down to you, as if I know something you do not, as if I've got it sorted and everyone else hasn't. I am no better than anyone else, and I will not let my words convince you otherwise. This is not a lecture; this is me coming clean. Let's start again.

I have a confession to make. It's quite a big deal for me to say it, because I've been trying to deny it for as long as I can remember. It's something I never wanted anyone to know, because I thought that if I believed it, everyone else would as well. But I can't keep up the façade any more. It's just too much. So here it goes, my confession.

I am not superhuman.

There, I said it. It's almost a relief to get it out in the open. It's been weighing me down for so long, the realisation that I'm not all I feel I should be. What a burden it has been.

I've struggled, you see, in trying to be the best at everything. I'm a perfectionist, a chronic high achiever. The world was my oyster, they said. The sky's the limit, or so I was told. I could do anything I wanted, if I put my mind to it. I saw opportunities wherever I went—opportunities to prove myself, to make myself better in the eyes of those around me; to get one step closer to becoming the person I'd always dreamed I'd be; to earn love and affection, praise and acceptance.

I wanted to be the best—and not just to be the best, but to be recognised as such. I wanted the world to see and hear and know just how good I was, just how I managed to do brilliantly in everything, have it all and still be in control. 'I don't know how she does it,' I wanted them to whisper as I passed. I wanted acceptance, I wanted accolades, I wanted the world at my feet.

But, as I clawed my way through life, I began to realise something. I learnt, step by step, that if I trod on people to get to the top, I would find myself frustrated and alone with no one to share my apparent success. If I placed my value in how well I did compared with those around me, I would never be truly satisfied. I realised that I was shutting down my humanity in order to succeed. Emotions became dangerous weaknesses. Control became my god, and perfectionism my lord and master. Trust was the first step towards failure. The thing was that no matter how well I did, it was never enough. Never was I good enough for my own high standards. Never was I satisfied. There was always something missing. There was always a hole left unfilled. I felt empty, desolate. I had a quiet longing, a yearning, for something more.

It's because I'm human, you see. I was created for something more than this world. I was created for more than degrees and promotions and human relationships. I was made in the image of the most high God and created for relationship with him. It is there, in my Father's arms, that I will find ultimate fulfilment. It is there that my brokenness becomes fullness of life. It is there that my wastelands will become like the garden of Eden. It is there that the pain I feel in the darkest nights of my life will turn to joy as the sun rises.

Trying to be superhuman doesn't work. I do not, and I cannot, keep the world going through my very existence. Trying to be perfect can, and will, destroy me. I am not invincible. I am not immune to pain. Emotions are not signs of weakness. Control is not something to hold on to, but something to relinquish. Trust is not the first step towards failure. Trust is the first step towards freedom.

And so, this is not just a confession, but a declaration.

I am not superhuman. And that is OK.

Why is it OK? Because I am hidden with Christ in God. I am a new creation. I am a joint heir with the Son of God himself. I do not have to earn or prove or achieve anything, for it is only by grace that I may enter. By the grace of God I am who I am, and I am fully satisfied within that grace. I am allowed not only to be in the presence of God, the very creator of the universe, but I may talk to him. I can boldly approach his throne, walk up to him, sit next to him and talk to him—ask for things; tell him everything I'm thinking, everything I'm feeling.

That confusion? I can talk it out with him. That pain? I can weep with him. That anger? I can rant at him. That anxiety? I can cast my burdens on to him. That fear? I can see it eclipsed by his perfect love for me. That weakness? I can see his power being made perfect through it.

I am not superhuman. But I am best friends with the king of the universe. It doesn't get much more super than that.

> For it is by grace you have been saved, through faith—and this is not from yourselves, it is the gift of God—not by works, so that no one can boast.
> EPHESIANS 2:8–9

Naked

For when you're feeling insecure

Tell me about yourself. No, not about your personality. Not about your likes or your dislikes. Not about your family or your school. Tell me about the actual physical you—your body. That thing which encases all those aspects of you that you're so eager to tell me about. That thing which, if you're honest, you don't really like. You try to ignore it as much as possible—or you try to beautify it and make it better, more aesthetically pleasing.

But answer me this: when was the last time you actually looked at yourself? I don't mean looking down as you stand there in your undies, quietly dismaying at this bit and wishing away that bit. I mean, when did you last stand naked in front of a mirror and look? And not just look, but gaze. Marvel. Stand in awe. Have you ever done that? Have you ever dared to stand naked and look?

We're constantly told that our bodies are only worth having, only worth showing off, if they're perfect—thin and toned and tanned and hairless. And if they're not, we'd best keep them under wraps, because 'Nobody wants to see that, do they, dear?' So we cover up. We don't look at ourselves, if we can help it, because our reflections won't be what we want to see. We avoid properly looking at our bodies in detail so that we don't have to be ashamed of all we are not.

But what if, instead of looking as the world looks, we looked as God looks. What if, instead of seeing all the things that are wrong, we saw all the things that are right? What if we looked at ourselves and marvelled at the complexity of what encases our very beings— the muscles, the curves, the tendons, the skin, the bones and the nerves? Look and see that you are 'fearfully and wonderfully made', that you were 'knit… together in [your] mother's womb' and are still being knitted now. You are growing and changing even as you read this book. Every single part of you—the seen, the unseen, the known, the unknown—is loved. And not just loved by anyone, but loved by its creator, the one who formed them. The one who formed the earth looks at you as his masterpiece, his prize possession. For you, you are made in the image of God.

So tell me again about yourself. You don't know? Take a look. Go, stand in front of the mirror and look. Gaze. Marvel. Stand in awe. Gaze at the beautiful creation that you are. Marvel at how you fit together. Stand in awe of how you're wrapped so beautifully into one being. Look at yourself—naked, without shame. Go on, I dare you. You never know what you might see.

> For you created my inmost being;
>   you knit me together in my mother's womb.
> I praise you because I am fearfully and wonderfully made;
>   your works are wonderful,
>   I know that full well.

PSALM 139:13–14

Out of the ashes

For when you need to be reminded of the beauty of redemption

You are running—running fast, running free. You are running like the wind, throwing off everything that entangles. You are running with the wind in your hair. You are running with perseverance and with faith.

But then, out of nowhere, comes a rope, a tripwire. Perhaps it's a word, a sentence, a doubt, an accusation, a memory, a flashback, a past pain, reignited, or former wound, reopened. It comes charging out of the wilderness and hits you full on. It takes you down, leaving you winded and shocked with no idea what to do. Looking around, you see you are sitting in the place you thought you'd left, long ago. You are sitting in the ashes of the grief of years gone by.

The ashes are still hot. Still they burn your face and your hands as you lie there, and you weep at the pain that still tears into your very being. Just one word, one memory, one conversation, one action, and you are back in the burning ashes of past hurts and the anger of injustice. The resentment and the bitterness still burns as you sit, wailing, in the ashes.

The sun goes down, and thoughts run through your mind, sparking doubts, creating questions. Why now, God? I was doing so well. Why this? You know how much it hurts. You know that this still burns. Can you not hear my cries? Can you not see the pain, the anguish? Why, O God, did you let me fall?

The darkness has come. All around you, people are running fast and free, but you are alone in the glowing embers, questioning, fearful and doubting; hurt, angry and alone.

Hours pass. Days, months, maybe even years go by as you sit in the ashes of yesterday's grief. Unsure of where to go next, dirty from the ashes that surround you, you feel as if you will never be rid of the dust that clings to every part of who you are. You are helpless in the ashes. In the darkness of the night, there is only weeping, and all you can see around are the remains of all that once was. It seems utterly hopeless.

But then, as you lament and question, ponder and weep, there appears a figure. Dazzling white, the brightness of his very being brings light into the darkness. Fearful, you shrink away. Is it really him, so bright, so clean, so holy? You scoot backwards across the ground, trying to get away, to protect him from the mess of your ashes. Such clean whiteness should be nowhere near such a stinking mess as the one in which you have dwelt for so long.

'No. Stop. Please don't come any closer.' You shun the brightness with words and actions, in fear that your darkness, your questions, your pain and your ashes will overwhelm and overcome the pure beauty of the one who approaches.

But still he comes. He draws ever closer to the mess in which you sit, until he is standing right beside you. You look up, expecting to see judgement, disgust or anger for the way in which you have acted, the way in which you have burnt and destroyed all that was given to you to look after. But as you look up, you see him kneeling down beside you, his pure white robe drawing close to you as he joins you on the ground.

But there is more than that. As he kneels, he begins to sweep. With his robe and with his nail-scarred hands, he scoops up the ashes that surround you. The embers that are still burning, he takes without flinching. And as he does this, he looks at you in a way you cannot begin to express. He looks with love, joy and adoration; forgiveness, acceptance and peace.

With the robe that he wears, he wipes the dirt from your face, from your hands and from your body, until he is filthy and you are clean. He looks away and towards the pile of ashes in front of him, the ones he has lovingly swept up at the expense of his own cleanliness. He looks at them and gathers up in those wounded hands the dirt and the mess and the burnt-up pieces that you tried to hide, over which you lamented and questioned, in which you were angry and bitter at the very one who now takes them on to himself.

Then, from the ashes, from the dirt and the grime, from the smelly, sticky, dirty fragments of all you have done and all that has been done to you—all the pain and the questioning, the lies, the fears and the wrongdoing—he makes something incredible. From the ashes he creates a masterpiece—a crown of the utmost beauty, the utmost splendour, fit only for the best of the best.

Holding the crown before him, he gazes upon you—you, dishevelled and snivelling; you, shaking and confused. He gazes upon you in complete and utter adoration. And gently, ever so gently, he places the crown upon your head. He places the crown upon your head and produces another pure white, dazzling robe, and with it he covers your trembling form. The ashes of yesterday are gone, and a crown of beauty adorns your head.

Undeservedly beautiful, unjustifiably pure, you get up off the ground and stand next to the one who took your ashes and gave you a crown in place of them. Holy and blameless, you stand with the one who came to you in your helplessness, in the darkest night, and brought hope to the hopeless. He turns and offers you his hand. And there, the place where you sat, dirty and alone, wailing and burning in the ashes of grief—it is there that you dance. You dance with the one who took the ashes you had made and replaced them with a crown of beauty.

As you dance, joy fills you. Incomparable, incomprehensible joy overwhelms your soul. You have been crowned as royalty by the King of kings. The dirty, smelly ashes in which you thought you would remain have gone for ever. Helpless and hopeless, you were met by the one who saves—the Redeemer—and he redeemed what you thought was irredeemable. Not only did he redeem it, but he made it beautiful. Through his sacrifice, the dirtying of himself with the filth of your ashes, you have been made clean and you have become whole.

[God has sent me] to provide for those who grieve in Zion—
to bestow on them a crown of beauty
    instead of ashes,
the oil of joy
    instead of mourning,
and a garment of praise
    instead of a spirit of despair.
ISAIAH 61:3

You turned my wailing into dancing;
    you removed my sackcloth and clothed me with joy.
PSALM 30:11

At the feet of Jesus

For when you don't know how to deal with your pain

I've always been scared of my pain. It seems unladylike, unnecessary and inconvenient. It gets in the way of getting things done, of being a 'functional adult', and often it also seems to get in the way of my faith. I will bring my carefully thought-out theological questions to God, approaching politely and quietly, and asking him calmly what he thinks. But these questions, these carefully thought-out theological questions, are not personal. They are abstract, distant and safe.

My pain, however, is personal. My pain is intimate to my life and it most certainly is not safe. My pain is uncontrollable and inexplicable. The questions surrounding my pain, the cries of 'Why?' and the wordless sobs are not so easily answered. These cannot be intellectualised, placed into an academic article or summarised neatly in a 3000-word essay. Pain cannot be brushed aside with 'You'll understand when you're older,' or 'It's going to be OK,' because you may never understand and it feels as if things will never be OK again.

I spent a lot of time hiding my pain from God. I expected to bring it to him and, in all honesty, I expected him to tell me to get over it. I expected human platitudes, a gentle but vaguely patronising pat on the arm, a metaphorical cup of tea and a reminder that there were other people in the world whose suffering was far worse than mine. I expected him to tell me to stop wasting his precious time, because he had other people to be looking after, other people with much more pressing issues and more acute pain than I could ever imagine.

But then I found myself at the feet of Jesus—alone in his throne room, my body heaving with sobs and my mind screaming the questions I had promised myself I would never ask.

'Why, God? Why then? Why that way? Why did we have to leave? Was it your will? Did you plan this? Did you call us to it? Were they really Christians? Were they really a part of your church, your body? Do you love me? Are you sure? Why did you let that happen? What about those we left behind? God, we had so much left to give, so much more to do. Why did you take us away? Why was she so sick? Why was he so angry? Why did you let that happen to a child? Why did they insist they were doing your will? God, I don't understand. God, it hurts. God, it still makes me so very, very angry. God, I'm still struggling to forgive. God, it still hits me when I least expect it, and I find myself on the floor, wounded and broken. God, if you are truly just and all-powerful, why did it happen? God, I don't understand.'

The questions went on and on, round and round, and the tears fell as they hadn't done for years. My shoulders shook uncontrollably, my fists clenched and my eyes shut.

And so I stood, at the throne of Jesus, of God, the king of the universe, and I cried.

There were no human platitudes. There were no metaphorical cups of tea. There were no reminders of the others who had suffered more than or differently from me. There were no gentle pats on the arm and no promises of later explanations or future understandings.

There was only acceptance—no words, no physical contact, no sympathetic sounds—just acceptance.

There was acceptance of the pain caused and the tears shed; acceptance of the time lost and the burdens carried; acceptance of me and my hurt; acceptance of the mess; acceptance of my sobs, and my anger, and my questions.

This response was not saying that what had happened was OK, that it was condoned or approved of. It was not a placation of me or an acceptance of the actions themselves, but an acceptance and a validation of the emotions caused by the actions. It was OK to be angry, hurt, confused, or to be questioning and begging for justice.

There weren't any answers. But there was something better. There was acceptance.

It was then that I began to lose the fear of my pain. It was there that I began to learn that God can cope with my tears, my anger, my deep-seated and overwhelmingly personal questions. It was at the throne of Jesus, with eyes closed, fists clenched and shoulders heaving, that I took another step towards letting go of all that had gone before.

You might be scared of your pain. It might be too unbearable even to utter. It might be so big and so strong that you fear it will tear you apart, should you even cast your eyes towards it.

Your pain might be scary to you, but it is not scary to the one who bore it 2000 years ago on that old, rugged cross. He took it upon himself to remove all that burdens you, shatters your confidence and destroys your trust. There is nothing too big for his shoulders to bear—even that which is too heavy for you to begin lifting. He will take it from you, and he will carry it.

There may not be answers, not this side of eternity. There may not be human justice. There may not be apologies, compensation or mediation.

But there will be acceptance, and it will be found at the feet of Jesus.

> In my distress I called to the Lord;
>   I cried to my God for help.
> From his temple he heard my voice;
>   my cry came before him, into his ears…
> He brought me out into a spacious place;
>   he rescued me because he delighted in me.
> PSALM 18:6, 19

Without words

For when you have no words
to express how you are feeling

What do you say when words are all you have, but words are not enough? Words may put names to your feelings but offer no respite; they may give coherence to your questions but offer no answers.

What happens when you no longer have the right words? The words that kept you afloat, described your thoughts and echoed your emotions—the words that were once closer than your own skin, that came tumbling out as easy as breath—are suddenly gone. No longer will words suffice for all that you are feeling, all that you are thinking, all that you are questioning. Words cannot depict the confusion of your mind and the turmoil of your emotions. Words will not change the situation in which you find yourself. Words will speak but they will not tell. Words will cry but they will not comfort. Words will seek but they will not find.

What do you say when everything is said? What do you write when the words on which you have always relied suddenly begin to fail you? Black ink on a white page becomes a poor imitation of all that you long to portray.

For the first time, words fail you.

What now? Where next? Where do you go when the words have disappeared, when things seem finished but feel so incomplete?

Be quiet for a minute. Clear your mind. Free it from the jumble of sounds, the mess of incomplete thoughts and unfinished sentences. Quieten your head and still your heart. Listen not for words, coherence or rhetoric. Search not for a thought to ponder or an idea to entertain. Just listen.

It is in the quietness that you find the freedom for which you have been searching. It is in the stopping, the stilling and the silencing that you realise you do not need words to explain who you are, how you are feeling or what you long to say. No longer must you paint a picture of words to explain your thoughts, for it is the silence that draws your soul to the surface. It is in the deep, soothing, overwhelming silence that your soul begins to sing. The peace permeates every fibre of your being as, slowly, words evaporate.

All that is left is you. There are no words to clothe you, no sentences to hide who you are. There is just silence—sweet, golden silence— and then, a whisper: a still small voice speaking in the silence. The voice of the creator is music, for it speaks truth to your very core.

There is truth to be found in the silence. There is hope to be found when words have failed. There is an understanding beyond language, a communication far greater than that of a human tongue. There is a depth of knowledge to be found when words fail. It comes in the form of a wordless whisper, in the silence of your very being.

Clear your mind. Quieten your head. Still your heart. And just listen.

> For God alone, O my soul, wait in silence,
>   for my hope is from him.
> PSALM 62:5 (ESV)

Heaven has a climbing frame

For when the cost of ministry is high

I think heaven has a climbing frame,
with multicoloured bars
attached to a bright-blue slide
and a fireman's pole hanging from the top.

The climbing frame can be a pirate ship,
a mountain,
a hiding place,
an adventure.
Its capacity is limited only
by a child's imagination.

It's the same as the one
we got when I was four,
a year before we moved
to a house with no garden.

It's the one that got sent to Hampshire
when we moved to Oxford
that I had to wait to play on
during our holidays
three times a year.

I think heaven has a swing set
with a sturdy wooden frame
and two swings swaying gently in the wind,
secured with ropes and chains.

The swing set makes you fly
until your feet
scrape the clouds above your head
and your heart is soothed
by the rhythm of the flight.

It's the same as the one
I bought with my birthday money
when I was twelve
before we moved, again.

It's the one I've never swung on.
Its frame is sat,
propped against our house,
unassembled
in our tiny London garden.

I think heaven has a trampoline
with green padding round the outside,
14 feet of bouncing potential
and a net, to keep you safe inside.

The trampoline gives you that feeling
of your tummy returning
to earth
just a few seconds
after the rest of you.

It's the same as the one
I got when I turned 15
that I bounced on for 16 months
before we moved once more.

It's the one that I lent to a friend
in the hope it would return,
but it was given to a stranger
because there was no longer
any room.

I don't really know if heaven
has a climbing frame,
a swing set
or a dark-green trampoline.

But I do know
that if it does not
it has something even better
because
God has seen, and he knows.

He sees what we have given up
and knows the sacrifices made
in order to do ministry
and to serve him in our lives.

He has promised to repay
the years the locusts have eaten,
and to give back tenfold
what we have left behind
in his service.

It may seem wrong
to dream of heaven having
worldly treasures and
earthly possessions.

*But I know that God
cares about the small things:
the letting go
and the saying goodbye;
the leaving behind
of things we have loved.*

*God didn't say that
serving him would be easy,
or that it wouldn't hurt
or require sacrifices.*

*But he did say that,
big or small pain,
he sees and knows.
He grieves
and he repays.*

*And so,
I think God cares about my climbing frame,
my swing set
and my trampoline
because I know
that God cares
about me.*

Jesus said to them… 'Everyone who has left houses or brothers or sisters or father or mother or wife or children or fields for my sake will receive a hundred times as much and will inherit eternal life. But many who are first will be last, and many who are last will be first.'

MATTHEW 19:28–30

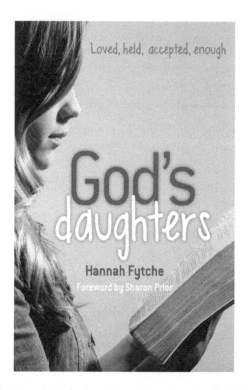

In this book, Hannah Fytche has taken six issues, each of which come with its own pressures: school, image, friends, family, church and your personal relationship with God. In each case you may feel that your teachers, family, friends or even God expects you to be better than you feel inside. You may feel that if you don't meet these expectations, you need to work harder in order to be loved and accepted. But this is not true! Her prayer for you is that you realise you have had enough of trying to be 'good enough'.

God's Daughters
Loved, held, accepted, enough
Hannah Fytche
978 0 85746 409 5 £6.99

brfonline.org.uk

In a series of pithy, poignant and profound short readings, this book explores the intersection of faith and life. Spotting parables in the everyday, it equips readers to explore whether they might be bumping into God without realising it. Heartening and often funny, it applies biblical truth in a way that both fascinates and liberates.

Could this be God?
Bumping into God in the everyday
Brian Harris
978 0 85746 500 9   £8.99

brfonline.org.uk

Ten inspirational stories to help churches and youth workers explore new approaches to mission and ministry to young people. Each section focuses on a particular initiative and includes a set of guidelines for how to apply the principles in your own context. There are sections on: Hanging around ministry; Sorted; The Feast; Rural bus ministry; Celebrate Life; The Lab; Wide Open; Hope MK; ConfiDANCE; and Messy Church.

Reaching Young People
New ideas for your youth ministry
Edited by Alex Taylor
978 0 85746 248 0 £8.99

brfonline.org.uk